MoneySmarts4U

by

Barbie O'Connor

Dedication

To Toby for all his love and support

For Danielle

and

Other girls like her

May you grow strong and prosper

Welcome

MoneySmarts4U is written for anyone who wants to improve his or her relationship with money. You may be starting out in life, graduating from high school, leaving college with a new degree, or you may be starting over after a divorce or the death of a loved one. Whatever your situation, *MoneySmarts4U*, can help you enhance your relationship with money.

Most people, especially your best friend, parents, or spouse, will be more willing to talk to you about sex than about money. Yet money---how well you manage it, how much you spend, how much you earn---will affect your life as much if not more than sex.

Each day there is a reading for your benefit regarding issues that affect your adult financial life. You can choose to read this book in the order laid out for you, or you can skip around to check out the topics that interest you the most. Each of the twelve chapters is designed to provide you information and provoke thought on your part about your life and how you want to live it.

Consider me a favorite aunt who cares about your success in life and wants the best for you. These stories and examples cover a different financial topic each day. When you are finished, I hope you will have a better understanding of the role money plays in your life and that you will appreciate money for what it is: a tool to give you the life you want.

I wish you the best for your future and hope MoneySmarts4U helps you be successful and happy throughout your life.

All my best,

Barbie

MoneySmarts4U: The Basics

Contents

Barbie O'Connor

Week One: Life Goals

When I talk about life goals during a seminar I like to draw a timeline on the chalkboard. One end is labeled "birth" and the other "death." Somewhere on the line, depending on the age of my audience, I make a mark labeled "You are here." From that point until death is the part of the line where I mention that what you do from this point, where you are right now, until death is totally up to you. Your choices and their outcomes will make a difference in the life you live, whether it is the life you want or one you just happen to create haphazardly as you go on down the road. Your life is totally up to you!

Day One

What Do I Want to Be When I Grow Up?

"What do you want to be when you grow up?"

How many times has someone asked you that since you were old enough to talk? At first you might have responded, "Fireman!" Or "Ballerina!" Maybe "Doctor" or "Policeman."

And now you may find that you still don't know what you want for yourself and your life, but you know you have to "be" something. Keep in mind you may go through at least six career changes during your lifetime. But "being" someone is more than just about your career or your job---it is about your lifework. It is about what is important to you and what matters to you, what your priorities are and what your present and future vision is regarding the time you spend on earth, known as your life. Each and every day is "your life."

Have you thought about that vision? Does it include being a solo adventurer with your entire life in a backpack you carry with you? Maybe you just want to carry a toothbrush and ID along with a little bit of money. Do you want to accumulate material goods? Do you want a fancy house? A lot of clothes? A car? These are questions to ask yourself.

Do you take responsibility for your actions? Can you take care of yourself? Not everyone remembers to eat regularly, attend to his or her personal hygiene, meet deadlines for school or work without resorting to elaborate excuses, or do their part of a team project without being reminded. Do you do what you say you will do? Or do you say yes without thinking or because you want to please others? Maybe you don't know how to say no. Do you or others think of you as responsible or irresponsible?

Are you interested in having a family, children, marriage and all the responsibilities that go with it? Are you willing to commit yourself to providing for others until they reach adulthood and possibly beyond? Do you understand the work and effort that goes into a lifelong partnership like marriage? Are you looking for a mate who is equally willing to do that work?

When you take the chance of marrying another person, consider that it may or may not work out between you. It takes two people to make a marriage work, and it takes two people to make a marriage fail. Although it is easier to point fingers at the other person, each party shares responsibility for success or failure of the relationship. If there are offspring from that marriage, will you be willing to raise these children yourself, with or without the financial, emotional, and physical support of your mate? Not sure? Then give your relationship more time and more tests before conceiving or adopting a child.

How long do you want to work in your life? Do you want to retire at forty, fifty, sixty or seventy years of age, or never? Do you want to factor in sabbaticals in your life, to allow time to learn new things? Would you like to have the time to evolve with the changing times? Need time for reflection to reinvent yourself or your profession or career? When you start your adult life, consider what you want to plan for at the middle and end of your life. Adjust your lifestyle accordingly.

Focus: Deciding what you want to be when you grow up depends a lot on your willingness to be responsible to yourself and to others.

Day Two
What Does Your Life Timeline
Look Like?

Think about the timeline of your life. Are you just now reaching eighteen years of age? Did you graduate from high school or get your GED? Is college on the horizon for you? Or are you considering trade or vocational school or a two-year certificate or degree program? Maybe you've already graduated from high school or college and are looking for your first job. There are so many things to think about during life and often it seems like we are playing a board game where we go in circles passing the same places over and over again.

As soon as the hormones in our bodies create desire for sex, the quest for a partner begins. Are you looking for a lifelong partner? A short-term relationship? Are you monogamous? Do you like to date around? What you choose will make a difference in your life as it plays out day to day. Are you in love or in lust? Can you tell the difference?

Do you want children? If not, do not engage in sexual intercourse without birth control. Take responsibility for preventing pregnancy before it happens. Use some form of birth control, like condoms, that both prevent conception and sexually transmitted diseases. If you are not sure about having children, wait until you can provide a consistent environment for them. Give them the best chance by creating a loving home for yourself, as well as for them. Don't look to your children to provide you with that love. Your job is to love them and care for them.

Want your children to go to college? Start a savings plan the minute they are born: 529 plans and Uniform Gift to Minors Accounts and educational trusts are available to you to make paying for that dream a reality. Contribute regularly to their college fund. Nurture your children's natural abilities, take pride in their accomplishments, tell them when they do a good job or achieve at a high level. Let them know you care for them and want them to be challenged and reach for the stars. When they fail, or don't succeed at the level they desire, remind them that everyone fails from time to time, and those who dust themselves off and get back on their feet and try again are those who eventually succeed. Share this with love and help them to carry your encouragement with them forever. Do the same for yourself.

What are your career ambitions? Do you have big dreams? Do you want to move around a lot as you make your way up the corporate ladder? Are the professions calling you? Doctor? Lawyer? Accountant? Teacher? Do you have a new idea that you plan to build a company around? Do you have a plan to achieve your ambitions? Remember to make friends along the way and take them with you as you rise in your career. Offer loyalty up and down the ladder of success.

Remember that someday if you raise children you may face the prospect of them leaving the nest. During this time of change, you will need to find your new self or maybe your old self, pre-children. Empty nesting is a time of renewal and evolution, a time when some of the same questions that applied when you grew into adulthood resurface for reexamination. What do you want to be when you grow up? How do you want to spend most of your time? At the same time your children may go through this type of self-examination, you, too, will be evaluating the vision of your life.

With people living longer, the care and attention diverted to aging parents is a major factor in the life timeline. Will there be in-home care or a retirement home? Will more frequent visits to the city where they live be required? Will your parents have to move to your city or into your home to be cared for properly? What will the added expenses be, and how can you plan for them?

What will your own retirement years be like? Will you move to a resort community and live in a condominium? Will you stay in your first home or the last home you lived in during your career? Will you live near your children or grandchildren? Will you be a volunteer? Learn a new skill or trade? Start another career? Follow your bliss? Grow your own food or live off the grid? What do you imagine you'd like your life to be like during your retirement years?

If you find yourself alone during the later, retirement years of your life, what will that be like for you? Will you consider it to be "me" time, time to rediscover yourself, what pleases you and what you dislike? Will you have a bucket list? Will other people be a part of your life? Will you still have friends from childhood? Will you make an effort to make new friends? Are they interested in the same things as you? How will you spend your time?

No one gets out of this world alive. We all die at some point or another. Some of us live to an old age and then die. But no one knows when or how that will happen until it does. How you age can be something you can manage, depending on your DNA. Your brain can only go where your body goes. Keep your body moving and your brain will follow. Simple but true. People who live long, healthy lives recommend walking every day—it keeps the body moving and it can clear your mind, preparing you for whatever is next in your life.

Focus: Our life timeline begins at birth and ends at death. Whatever you do in between is defined as "your life." Make the most of it! There are lots of points along the way for renewal and reconsideration. If you don't like your life right now, then change it. You are the only one who can make a difference in "your life."

Day Three
Self-Awareness

Looking up into the sky, blue and dotted with different-shaped clouds, have you ever let your mind wander, to imagine different possibilities of what your life might be like, to consider happiness?

Sometimes you might get the idea that happiness comes only after something else has happened in our lives. "I'll be happy after I get married." Or "I'll be happy after I have a big house." Or "I'll be happy after I get this jerk out of my life." Thinking like that puts your happiness in the hands of other people and external events. Simplifying your happiness to what is essential to you and to what is in your power to obtain, create, or maintain will help you with planning throughout your life.

What is important to you? Fancy cars? Expensive jewelry? Following fashion? Spending time with others? Living in a big house? Enjoying nature? Spending time alone? Staying busy? Traveling? Bossing people around? Learning from others? Learning on your own? Does freedom matter to you? Do you prefer to have others make choices for you, or do you want to make your own decisions? Knowing what matters to YOU, not to your parents or your friends, will provide you compass points for so many decisions to make in the future.

Living in a small apartment may free up more time for you to travel or let you have more personal luxuries, like fine wine, good chocolate, designer clothes, or important art, whereas a large house comes with another set of obligations like more maintenance, furnishings, a yard, more space, more responsibility. A high-performance sports car usually costs more to begin with, in addition to using more fuel and having higher maintenance costs. Does the pleasure you receive from the decisions you make affirm your desires for your life? Do you feel you make the right decisions for you?

Sometimes when you are not sure what you want, you may sabotage yourself. When you go on a diet to lose ten pounds, are you doing it for yourself, or for your boyfriend? Are you the motivation behind that decision? Are you doing it because it is good for your health, because it will make you feel better about yourself, and because you have a responsibility to yourself to lose that weight? Most likely when a diet fails, or you don't do your homework, or you miss a deadline, it is because you aren't completely sold on the idea behind the commitment. Or because you decide that something else is more important to you. You have a slice of birthday cake even though you are on a diet, because you want to participate in the party and celebrate with the birthday boy or girl.

Sometimes you procrastinate and don't study for the test or do the homework you need to do. You want to watch TV with your family or friends rather than do your homework because you want to be with them more than you want to be by yourself doing math problems or writing an English paper. By allowing your immediate needs to be met rather than thinking about how good it will feel to finish the homework well, or make a passing grade on the test or obtain a high grade-point average that will help you get into college or graduate school, you get confused about your priorities and give yourself immediate pleasure rather than long-term happiness.

By procrastinating you may be punishing yourself. By not honoring your commitments to yourself, you may feel like you are letting yourself down. After all, if you can't keep promises you make to yourself, do your promises mean anything at all? Being true to yourself will lead you to understand your own priorities, be able to act on them, and meet your own needs, which ultimately will bring you happiness.

If you don't know what you want, because maybe you were never given a chance to make choices on your own, and you are now just discovering that once you become an adult you are responsible for the consequences of your choices, then start thinking about what matters to you, and take small baby steps toward making your own decisions.

Small steps involve keeping a "Decision Diary," where you document all the decisions made for you or by you during a day, from what time you wake up in the morning even the food you eat, the work you do, the people you interact with and how you do that, to how you prepare yourself for going to sleep at night. Being aware of how you live your life can help you in the future. Do you procrastinate? Do you go along to get along? Do you do what your parents tell you to do, without evaluating those "orders"? Are you respectful of yourself and others? Are you pleasant and courteous, or are you just concerned for yourself? If you feel writing this down would be too time consuming, then at least once an hour take about five minutes to review your behavior and choices during the previous hour. Are you meeting your commitments to yourself? Have you acted with your own best interests at heart?

Focus: Get to know yourself. What are your most important needs? Are you making decisions that fulfill those needs? Think about what matters to you. What are your values? What is your code of life based on? Be true to yourself. Listen to your gut response to people, places, and events. Pay attention to your feelings.

Day Four

What Are Your Priorities?

As much fun as it would be to be able to do whatever you want whenever you want, that is just not possible. You have to set limits and boundaries: limits on how much time you can exercise each day, on how much money you can spend on gifts and presents, on how much you can do for others, on how much food you can eat, on what you can do to help those less fortunate than yourself. You can only do and be so much. Learning how to set those limits and boundaries is one of the toughest tasks in your life, but one of the most loving gifts you can give to yourself and to others.

Time is your most valuable asset. There is no way to make up for time you waste or spend in a way you believe is wasteful. Clarifying the value of time to you is priceless.

What do you most like to do with your time? Spend it with other people? Do something active? Learn something? Create something? Do something passive? Work on a friendship? Deepen a relationship? Use it to invest in your future? It really is up to you, but how you spend your time will affect so much of your day-to-day life.

Maybe you think watching television is a foolish use of time, but if you are watching a sporting event with your dad, especially one he truly is passionate about, then maybe what you are doing is really spending time with Dad, not watching television. Maybe the next time you get together with your dad you can do something you like to do----work in the garden say, or play chess or bake bread or go to the park. Setting limits and boundaries with your family and friends can make your lives more interesting together, especially if you negotiate to alternate who chooses what to do. By telling your dad that maybe it would be good to do something different together, something you would enjoy, you might enable him to have a new experience in his life. You've set limits i.e., Dad doesn't always get his way and you've established boundaries i.e. our relationship needs to be about my interests as well as yours.

Every day involves obligations you are required to fulfill if you want to keep your life in some semblance of order. Are you making time for those obligations? Are you eating regularly?

Exercising? Paying your bills? Spending time with friends? Doing your homework? Studying for a test? Returning phone calls? Responding to text messages? Checking your emails? Cleaning your bathroom? Changing your sheets? Doing laundry? Staying in touch with family?

Beyond these mundane activities that you have to do, what else do you want to spend time doing? Do you want to restore an old car? Are you looking for the love of your life? Is there a show at the museum that you want to see? Are picnics at a local park a treat for you? Do you and your dog like to explore new paths on your daily walks? Is reading a passion of yours? Have you wanted to learn to paint in watercolors? Learn to focus on what is important to you and to make the time for those activities. Life will have greater satisfaction for you.

Once you have learned more about your own priorities, it gets a lot easier to make decisions about time and about money. Why spend money on going to the movies if you fidget all the way through the main feature? Why not go dancing with a group of friends and learn to salsa while you catch up with each other? Finding the love of your life might happen if you go places and do things that YOU really like to spend time and money doing. Knowing the order of importance of those events or causes will simplify decisions during your life when time or money is scarce. You'll know what is first on the list and what is last as well.

Throughout your lifetime, your priorities will change. If you marry, your spouse will become more important than your parents. Any children will become secondary to your spouse, although it will be a very close second, but that will change your priorities for how you spend and invest your money. Each year, around your birthday or at the New Year, consider a personal priority inventory, to see how things have changed in your view and your life. A family meeting might yield a joint vision of family priorities. Illness in the family, a divorce, a move to another city, a new job, or a new member of the family will change your personal priorities, especially if you are directly affected by the new factor.

Focus: How you spend your time is how you spend your life. Think about whether you are meeting your priorities in how you spend your time and your money. How could you be more true to yourself with your time and money each day?

Day Five
Opportunity Costs

Time is the one asset you never get back once you spend it. It's easy to realize that if you spend time going to a movie with a group of friends, you can't spend that same time with your grandma baking cookies. That's why waiting by the phone for the right person to call you to go do something is so infuriating—because you can't get that time back. The same thing happens when you refuse invitations because you are hoping for another one, a better one, to come your way. If you do so you can find yourself with nothing to do and no place to go.

The same issues apply to money. If you spend money to go to the movies, you might not have the money you need to pay your car payment. If you don't make your car payments, say goodbye to your car and hello to the repo man who comes and takes it away. There is a cost to the financial decisions we make, known as "opportunity cost."

If you spend money or time on one thing, it may not be available for something else that is more important to you. Want to go to Europe and travel the Continent next summer? In order to do so you may have to save that money now, not spend it on eating out or partying with your friends. Getting up early to make a job fair so you can get a job means you can't sleep late. If you do one thing, then you give up another.

If you impulsively spend money on the latest fashions or newest gadgets, you may not have the money later when you want it to buy a car or take a trip somewhere to get out of town. Thinking about how you spend your time and your money now will give you more opportunities later.

Focus: Think about your actions and decisions and the opportunity cost related to those choices. Remember, your life timeline is a long one, and you build your life one decision at a time.

Day Six

When Life Throws You Curveballs

We all make mistakes. None of us are perfect. Things happen in life that don't go as planned or don't have a happy ending. Pay attention to how you feel when life is handing you problems. Forgive yourself if you are failing or not living up to your own expectations. Learn from your mistakes. Be grateful for all the good in your life—family, friends, home, spiritual life, whatever abundance your life holds. Also, be thankful for any problem you are facing. It is there to teach you something, to give you a chance to be stronger, to learn from the experience, to become a better person. Obviously, when you are in the middle of a lot of pain it is very hard to see the benefit of your situation, but if you can do so, it will make life better for you.

Needless to say, the curveballs in life can play havoc with your finances. Losing your job leads you to ask, "Where is the money going to come from to pay my day-to-day bills? To put food on my table? To pay the electric bill? To buy medicine for my children?" Creating a nest egg and an emergency fund of six to nine months worth of expenses can make losing your job less stressful, but it cannot assuage the emotional hit your ego will take if this happens to you.

If you lose your job, approach the people you know, your network, about helping you find another one. If nothing else, friends and family can be a great support group. Who knows---someone may actually know of a job opening somewhere. The saying "It's who you know, not what you know" refers to getting you in the door of a new business, and most of the time it is very true. What you know is what will allow you to shine once that door to a new job is open. Keep in touch with friends and business colleagues to create a network that is there for you when you need it.

A serious illness like cancer, depression, or alcoholism often requires good medical help, a network of friends, and a willingness to change your lifestyle to improve the status of your health. Often group therapy programs can help the afflicted as well as family members cope with the physical, emotional, spiritual, and financial strain of a difficult long illness. Remember to ask for help. Don't try to go it alone. Use the resources available to you from your community and the health care system.

Unexpected pregnancies are just that: unexpected. How a woman deals with it is her decision. A woman can raise the child, put it up for adoption, abandon the child at a fire or police station with no legal consequences under the Safe Haven Law also known as the Baby Moses law, or abort the fetus during the legal time limit currently allowed by law in the United States. Each individual decision has a consequence of its own, so evaluate and choose carefully how you will handle the unexpected. Raising children is a long-term and expensive proposition. The United States Department of Agriculture's cost estimates for raising a child between birth and eighteen years of age fall between $221,000 and $277,000, taking into account medical care, education, food, clothing, and housing for all of those years. Planning for pregnancy means planning finances as well. This is a very important issue to consider when you plan to start a family.

Not all curveballs in life have negative implications. A sudden windfall through inheritance or luck can be a blessing for your present as well as your future. When you have a plan for your finances, then you can employ this money in a way that builds your emergency fund or adds to your long-term investment account for something you wanted or planned to purchase later on in life. A giving plan incorporated within your spending plan allows you to thoughtfully consider charitable gifts you want to make with your earnings or with a portion of a windfall you may receive. With a spending and saving plan, you may even be able to treat yourself to something fabulous if a windfall comes your way.

You may have dreams of something you want to do or be that requires taking a chance on yourself. Maybe you want to go back to school, or maybe you want to start a new business, or maybe you want to create or invent something. Your dreams may not bear fruit, in which case you may have to start over again----or you could be wildly successful. Until you take that chance, you will never know. If taking time off to pursue this dream is part of your spending and saving plan, then you can do so with confidence. If it comes about due to a lost job or an illness or other interruption in life, then move forward with it. If it doesn't work out, then forgive yourself, remembering that you did explore your dream and your potential, then move on to the next chapter in your life

Focus: Plan for the worst and hope for the best. A spending and savings plan incorporating an emergency fund and six or nine months worth of expenses can help make the bumps in the road of life a bit smoother.

Day Seven
Putting It All Together

It is very easy to allow life events to sweep you away from what matters to you personally. Early in life, peer pressure can put you in situations that can change your life forever. Being mindful of your values and your aspirations can make a difference in your future.

Take the time right now to make a list of the five people you love the most, the people whose absences, if they were gone tomorrow, would create great sadness in your life. Make a note of when the last time was that you saw them or had a long conversation with them. If you've seen them in the last month, congratulations!--you have your people

25

priorities straight. If not, ask yourself why not, and then do what you can to maintain contact and gain wisdom and love from these very special people in your life.

Now, make a list of the five activities you enjoy the most. Again, list the last time you participated in that activity. If it has been a while, then evaluate why that is. Cost too much? Weather has been bad? Can't make the time? Others have been selecting the activities of your life? What do you need to do to prioritize the activities that matter to you?

Finally, make a list of the five qualities or values that matter the most to you. How are you living your life to exemplify those values or qualities? Are you self-absorbed? Caring? Generous? Helpful? Self-centered? Empathetic? Irresponsible? Considerate? What do you need to do to change the way you are living in order to live according to your values and priorities?

Focus: This is your life. Your values and priorities will determine how it plays out. Knowing who matters in your life and what is important to you will make planning your future and your finances much easier. Knowing your needs versus your wants will simplify your decision-making. Realizing that time is the one asset you never get back in life will help you make better decisions about how you spend your time. Every year revisit your values, priorities, people who matter, things you like to do, and your spending and savings plans. Are you spending your money and your time on the people who matter and the things you like to do? Are you honoring your values and your priorities?

Life Goals

1. Think about what you want your life to be like, how willing you are to be responsible to others and yourself.

2. Remember that you are in charge of your own life. You can make a difference in how you live each day.

3. Get to know yourself. Learn the difference between your needs and your wants.

4. Be aware of the code of life you want to live by and what your values are.

5. Pay attention to your feelings, your gut response to people, places, and events.

6. Be true to yourself. Act with your best interests at heart.

7. Make a list of the opportunity costs of your time, your actions, and your decisions for today.

8. Have a plan for life's curveballs. Save for your nest egg and for your emergency fund.

9. If you need help with any disappointments, pain, or failures in your life, ask for it.

10. See the people you love, do the things you like to do, develop the qualities and values in yourself that are your life code.

Week Two: Getting Around Town

When I was a teenager, the first job I had required me to go downtown from our house in the suburbs. Since I did not have a driver's license, I took the bus. I walked about two blocks to wait for the bus that traveled down a major thoroughfare, taking me directly downtown. From there I walked one block to the building where I worked. Coming home, I had to walk about six blocks if I left work later and caught a different bus. It was cheap, safe, and so easy.

After a few weeks I knew the other regular riders on the bus, and they looked out for me, asking the bus driver to wait when I was running late to catch the bus. On my way to work or back home, I'd read, think about what I had to do later in the day, or daydream as I stared out the window. Later in life, whenever I was looking for a place to live, I always looked for the nearest bus stop, and checked the bus schedule for the route that might take me closest to work. Early in my career, I regularly took the bus to work, unless I had an appointment late in the day with a client and would need a car to get there.

Day One
Hiking, Biking, Trains, Planes, and Automobiles

Choose the best way to get to work, school or around town that is best for you. From mopeds and minicars to bicycles, buses, trains, and subways, there are lots of choices. Some cities have great walkability scores and offer many mass transit choices, while others require a car. You may find that a combination of transportation methods suits your lifestyle and may give you extra benefits besides saving money. You may feel virtuous because you are conserving energy, protecting the environment, getting more exercise, losing weight, and eating local. Consider your transportation choice when you select a place to live as well as the companies where you want to work. Many employers get involved with their communities to make more methods of transportation affordable and available to their workforce.

Most large cities have well-designed bus, trolley, or streetcar systems designed to help with long commutes via a park-and-ride program, or to allow for an easy trek across town. A monthly pass will be cheaper than a day-by-day rate and may give you unlimited trips on a community system. Passes may include discounts for local commuter trains or subway routes too.

Learning to use a mass transit system can be a big help if you travel abroad or if you travel for business or for school. Learning how to read the timetable charts and connection maps and to discern the different routes possible for the destination you are looking for is a skill that can pay off financially and enhance your experience in a new and different community.

In some cities there are car-sharing systems that allow you to rent a small car for a few hours when you need it simply by reserving it and paying for it online. If you need a car only occasionally, this system might be worth looking into for those few times.

Owning your own motorized transportation, whether a moped, motorcycle, or automobile, comes with additional expenses beyond a monthly transit system pass or occasional taxi ride. Parking fees, gas, oil, tires, insurance, cleaning fees, and other repair costs are part of owning a vehicle. In addition, you must obtain and pay for a driver's license particular to the type of motorized vehicle you want to drive, and also pay for an annual inspection and license fee to the state where the vehicle is registered. A motorized vehicle may give you more independence, but you may find yourself in traffic jams and experience added frustrations when you drive, since you have to deal with other motorists and potential accidents.

If you live in a community where you must have a car, ask your insurance agent about a discount on your coverage if you take a defensive driving course. They may offer other incentive programs based on your driving record or other factors. To preserve the value of your car engine, change the oil as instructed by the manufacturer or every year or every three thousand miles, whichever comes first. Properly inflating your tires using the pressure information found on the driver's door or in the manual will give you better gas mileage, and better control over your vehicle and will keep you apprised of the condition of your tires. The only thing between you and the pavement is your tires, so replace them when they are worn. Washing, vacuuming, and cleaning the interior of your car will also extend the life of your vehicle and make it more attractive as a trade-in or at resale when it comes time to replace it or get rid of it.

Focus: Consider self-propelled methods of travel, as well as mass transit in order to save money for other spending plan categories.

Day Two
What Will It Cost?

Walking to class or work, to run errands or pick up groceries will be the least expensive option available to you. Your biggest investment will be a good pair of walking shoes. Beyond that, a raincoat, umbrella and shopping bag---items you already have---will be the extent of your expenses if walking is your main method of transportation. Allowing sufficient time to get where you are going is another consideration when walking to your destination.

Biking involves purchasing the appropriate bike that is comfortable for the route you will normally take. Used bikes can be found at thrift shops, pawnshops, or estate and garage sales. Additional expenses will be a helmet, a basket, saddlebags, or a backpack.

Taking mass transit usually involves a daily fee or a monthly pass giving you the freedom to roam the entire system. Familiarize yourself with the bus/train/subway routes and stops before you start your semester or your first day of work. You may want to leave a bit earlier to make sure you can catch the bus, train, trolley, subway, or streetcar in a timely fashion. If the train or bus is full and you have to wait for the next one that comes along you may be late for class or work.

Before you can purchase a motorized vehicle like a motorcycle, moped, or automobile, you will need to take a driving course as mandated by law in the state where you live. A specific number of hours of classroom instruction will acquaint you with the laws that apply to driving in preparation for the written portion of the driving test. Once you pass the written part of the test, which entitles you to a "learner's permit," you will then commence the in-car portion of driver training. These in-car driving classes give you experience on the road for anywhere from ten to twenty hours behind the wheel before you are permitted to take the in-car driving test. Various car clubs offer enhanced driving skill development classes that teach emergency responses and controlling a car going into a skid. These enhanced classes use simulators or operate on closed driving courses, providing valuable added experience for young or novice drivers before heading out on the road. Each state has its own rules regarding licensing, so when you move to a new state, review the laws that govern driving and licensure in that area. Once you have a driver's license, you can begin the process of buying a motor vehicle. In many states, proof of insurance is required before you can test-drive or buy a vehicle.

I was twenty-four years old when I finally saved enough money to buy the car of my dreams: a white Fiat convertible with a black top and red leather interior. I felt like a celebrity when I drove that car. With a standard transmission and a stick shift, it took a little while for me to learn not to stall the car while using both the clutch and the brake when I stopped for traffic signals, especially when I was stopped on a hill. The first day I had the car, I was so proud that I'd saved enough money to buy a new one that I took it over to show my Dad. Yes, he was impressed that I'd saved so much money, that I bought it outright with no payments, and that it was such a sexy, sporty little car. However, when I took him for a spin around the neighborhood, I stalled it at the stop sign at the corner nearest our house. While I was furiously trying to start it again, he turned to me and said, "I can't believe you bought a car you can't even drive!" Needless to say, I still love cars with a stick and drive one to this day. You can have the vehicle of your dreams if you save for it, but just remember you may have to learn new skills to drive it.

A moped or motorcycle will be less expensive than most cars. They use less gas but are faster than riding a bicycle or walking. Taking a motorcycle safety class before you buy a motorbike may get you a discount on your insurance, as well as familiarize you with safer driving techniques. Additional protective gear may be a worthwhile investment to protect your face, skin, and clothes from road rash, bugs, sun, and windburn. Many car drivers have difficulty seeing motorcyclists and mopeds on the road, so be cautious and drive defensively. Additional costs will include a driver's license and registration fees.

An automobile can be purchased new or used through brand dealerships throughout the country. Often a dealership will certify a used-car and give it an extended warranty, providing an advantage to the used-car buyer. If you are looking for a daily driver that works but is cheap to run, then you may find a used-car is your most economical option.

New cars have the appeal of having all the latest gadgets, that new-car smell, and a new-car warranty that may include a service contract for a three-year or five-year period. Unfortunately, when you buy a new car and drive it out of the dealership the resale value drops about ten percent to twenty percent immediately. Usually buying a new car will be the most expensive transportation option.

Focus: Work to match your budget to your transportation needs, considering all of the expenses involved.

Day Three
Buying a New Vehicle

You may have the desire for a car you've seen in an ad or watched roar away in a movie. Your imagined perfect car may be part of who you envision yourself becoming. Even though there may be one brand that you fixate on, there may be other, less expensive ones that can give you the same features, the same versatility, and the same or better thrill that you imagine. Research, test drive, stay in your budget, and then negotiate for the best deal you can get.

Before you buy a vehicle, whether it is a moped, motorcycle, or car, research the features you want on it. After you figure out the features you want, then study evaluations of the brands and models. Most auto magazines like *Car and Driver* or *Motor Trend* will come out with a rating grid of all the new cars on the market, available in print or online. Another source of information regarding repair records is *Consumer Reports.* You may have your heart set on a certain model and make, but if you find that it spends more time in the shop than on the road, you may want to revise your selection. Another source of information is online resale websites like *Auto Trader.* There may be ten to twenty sale listings for a car make, model, and year, possibly indicating there is a problem with the design or manufacturing for that year. Often the first year of a new car model might have a few design glitches that are corrected in later production models. Find out when the "new" model started and avoid that year.

The more gadgets you put on your car, the more expensive it will be and the more things can break. If you absolutely have to buy a new car, then consider whether you need all the bells and whistles you've selected or found on the cars at the dealership. Many of the new electronic navigation systems require updates annually to keep the mapping information fresh, so factor in that expense as you think about the annual cost of owning a car. Vehicles offering concierge services or satellite radio may require a monthly fee to maintain the availability of those services for your car. Sometimes your cell phone offers the same maps, concierge services, or genre radio stations already included in your monthly billing package, so paying for it a second time may not be necessary if you are looking to save money each month.

Before you walk into the dealership to negotiate for a new car, review online inventory at various dealerships around your state to see if what you want is shown there. Many dealerships give an online purchase discount to buyers immediately. Although your local dealer can swap a local car for one in another city or state, they make more money on what they already have in their inventory.

It's better to pay cash for a car than to pay for one with monthly payments, unless you can be assured that your income stream will cover your payments for the three-year or five-year period the financing contract endures. Remember, the interest you are paying adds to the cost of the car, so do a little math before you agree to finance terms. Make sure you understand the contract, the terms of payment, the definitions of "default" or "in arrears", and the consequences of failure to pay for the car.

One would be better off paying cash for a used car that is in good condition than financing a vehicle with monthly payments.

When you plan to pay cash for a vehicle, do some homework before you go into the store, and be prepared to walk out and walk away from the car you are dying to buy. Don't fall in love with the car of your dreams. If you do, you'll pay too much for it and later will regret that. Look for the car's MSRP----the Manufacturers Suggested Retail Price, usually found as the bottom line of the sticker price. However, dealers have started adding on various extras to make the price higher and to enhance their profit margins. These include special protective paint coatings, special floor mats, insurance for tires or rims, and anything else they can create to get you to pay them more. Many of these specialty items are not already on the car but are put on the car or the contract at the time you make the deal, so ask about all of the extras and what they mean and whether they are already part of the vehicle. In addition, usually state sales tax is levied on the purchase price or the difference between the purchase price and a trade-in vehicle valuation. Licensing fees, registration fees, and make-ready fees are also added to the total you pay for a new car. Many "packages" offered on cars may include extras you really want, along with something you don't care a hoot about, but if you order a car it will cost you more to go "a la carte" than to buy the package as it is put together on the menu of options.

Once you've figured out the price range of the automobile you are looking to buy, have a strategy when you go in to the dealership. Go in during the third or fourth week of the month. Salespeople have to make a quota each month. Help them do it. Right before the new models come out, in August or September, there are often sales on the previous year's models. There may also be sales right before year-end, in December, since many states tax businesses on the value of their year-end inventory. Make sure you are well rested and well fed when you go in. Wear comfortable clothing and shoes; take something to read or occupy your time, so you can stay busy during the wait times while the salesman and sales manager try to wear you down.

Decide how much time you have to spend on this purchase. If you are going to test drive, then plan on spending at least three to five hours on the total package of the test drive, haggling stage, and paperwork. You may want to test-drive vehicles on a previous visit to the showroom, before you decide which car to buy. Tell the salesperson how much time you have to start with when you begin the dance of buying a car.

Keep in mind that whatever you say while in the dealership, during the test drive, or in the sales office may be overheard or listened to by the sales manager or salesperson, so don't talk about how much you want the car, or the maximum you would be willing to pay. Beware of Wi-Fi networks that may be on too, keeping track of any texts or emails you might send with negotiating strategies you want to clear with another person. Be prepared to notify the salesperson that your time is up and that you plan to walk out the door, especially if the deal is still in play.

Once, when helping a friend buy the car she wanted, I had to drag her out of the dealership because the sales staff was not working with her. She was in tears as she left, sure that her dream car was going to be gone the next day. Shortly after she arrived home that evening, she listened to a message from the dealership stating that she could buy the car for the price she wanted to pay. Remember: when you walk out the door, the transaction walks out with you, and the sales commission too.

If you have seen similar cars online, then make sure you have that data with you, you may want to use it as part of your bargaining strategy. Start your negotiating price at fifteen percent below the MSRP bottom line figure. If the car you are buying is popular, then you may want to start at ten percent below. You can always go up in price, but not down. Sales commission is about six percent of the total, so you have about nine percent to play with when negotiating with the car salesman and the sales manager. State tax and licensing fees usually are about ten percent of the total price without taking the trade-in into account. These will be added on to the price you settle on during negotiations.

If the car is listed at $35,000, then you will want to start out at $29,750. The sales person will say no, countering with another amount, say $34,000. Usually negotiations go back and forth three times before you are told that is the best price for the car. When you counter the second time, decide whether you want to go further. If not, tell the salesman that is your final offer. Some buyers decide what they will pay and present it to the salesperson at the beginning as the best they will do, usually offering about seven percent below the sticker, so once the tax, title, and license are paid for they end up at MSRP. If the deal is refused, they walk out the door. Figure out the strategy that feels most comfortable to you, and then work with it.

Remember to be nice while you are going through this process. Most salespeople in the car business either move up in the dealership where they start out, or they move around from dealership to dealership, so you may run into them again sometime. That is not to say that you can't be assertive and firm, but do it with a smile on your face, and a kind goodbye. You can be a tough negotiator and still get your dream car at the price you can afford and are willing to pay.

Focus: Know the model car you want, the features you want, and the price you are willing to pay, and have a strategy for arriving at that number, knowing you will have to haggle to get the car you want.

Day Four
Buying a Used Car

With the advent of dealer warranties on certified used cars, savvy buyers can acquire a "cream puff" of a used car at a reasonable price without the automatic devaluation that may occur the minute you drive a new car off the dealership lot. Some dealerships specialize in used cars, offering every make and model imaginable, many only a few years old. Dealerships often certify used cars that were part of the leasing fleet. Demonstrator models including the dealer owner's car may fit into the "not new but barely used" category, with a discounted price. With most leases running three years, there are additional cars every month, providing a regular inventory of vehicles for the dealership to sell as pre-owned vehicles. Records of the accident histories of these cars, plus in many cases the repair and service records may be available online or at the dealership. Before buying a certified used car with an additional warranty, make sure you understand what the warranty covers and where the repairs must take place to maintain the warranty as beneficial for your use.

Most of the rental car companies----Hertz, Avis, Alamo, National, and others----have sales on their rental cars as they rotate new models into their fleet. Although these cars may have been through a lot during their short lifespan, with careful evaluation you might find a diamond amid the vehicles they have to offer. Since some of these companies only offer certain brand-name vehicles, they may partner with that brand to offer extended warranties or certification for the cars they are selling from their fleet.

Prepare for buying a used car just like you would for a new car. Do the research; figure out what you want, what you are willing to pay, and what the market price appears to be online. Check the *Kelly Blue Book* website for values on similar vehicle makes, models, and years. Remember that once a car is over five years old, it may not be eligible for financing, and then only buyers who have cash will be able to buy that vehicle, or it will only serve as a trade-in for another car. Cars over five years old should be deeply discounted in price, even if they are in great shape, simply because many people don't have the cash to buy a car.

If you know a good mechanic or a repair shop that comes well recommended, you may want to have the car checked before you buy it. Mechanics who specialize in certain makes can often tell you what repairs and parts replacement will be needed as the vehicle ages. Obviously, a mechanic is not a fortune teller, but he or she can usually tell the vehicle has been well-maintained mechanically, giving you insight as to whether it has "good bones" or not.

Focus: Buying a quality used car may give you the best bang for your buck. It allows you to avoid automatic depreciation in value and may enable you to afford more luxury for the amount you've budgeted for your vehicle.

Day Five

Leasing a Vehicle

If you can't quite afford the car you are looking at, don't fall for the temptation of a lease on the car. Leases were designed for businesses to take advantage of a loophole in the tax law that allows a tax deduction of the lease payments for a vehicle used in or for business. Recently they've been enhanced to tempt buyers who can't afford to buy a new car to sign a lease agreement. The sales pitch involves the line "You can get a new car every three years for less."

Usually the lease involves a large down payment that offsets the depreciation of driving the car out the door, along with monthly payments and strict requirements to comply with maintenance agreements and vehicle condition specifications for the three or five years of the lease. If you change your mind about the car, you can't sell your way out of the lease without making penalty payments. But if you pay cash for a car or buy it with monthly payments, then it's yours to do whatever you'd like with it.

Lease agreements can work for people who are careful drivers and keep their cars clean and tidy, as they will have little to worry about when the car is turned in to the dealership at the end of the lease. Others, who might be more careless or messy, might have penalty fees to pay. Lease agreements provide some businesspeople with the benefit of deductions for the lease payments and a facility for trading up to a new vehicle every three years, with the option of buying that vehicle for a specified price. Usually the overall cost of the car is greater with a lease if the purchase option is selected. Doing the math to calculate just what it will cost you to lease a car over the lifetime of the lease is important before you sign the paperwork and enter into the agreement.

Focus: Before entering into a long-term lease agreement for a vehicle, make sure you know and understand the terms of the agreement and the total cost to you. You may find that buying a used car or even a new one is a better decision.

Day Six

Renting a Car

When your car is in the shop, when you go on vacation, or when you are traveling on business, it may be necessary to rent a car for the period you are away from home or inconvenienced. Rental car contracts are rife with extra fees, so be careful when you make your rental reservations, and read the contract before you drive off in the car you are renting.

Rental companies offer navigation systems and concierge services for a fee. These are obviously optional: your cell phone may offer something similar. You can buy gas ahead of time, too, so before you agree to that cost, find out how much gas costs in that area and whether you will be charged for an entire tank or by the gallon when you bring it back. If you are responsible for turning the car back in with a full tank, then pay attention to the locations of gas stations close to the rental car return so you can fill up before you miss your opportunity and find charges for gas on your bill.

Most controversy arises from the issue of buying insurance from the rental car company. You can pay for the insurance offered by the company, which usually is about twenty-two dollars to thirty-five dollars a day for all the insurance: insurance on the car, on other people's cars, for your body, and for other people's bodies. This insurance takes care of everything: legal fees if you have to go to trial, repair and replacement of the vehicle, medical expenses for anyone who is injured, and so on. Yes, it is high, but it may be well worth the price. If you rent a car for ten days, then you may pay three hundred and fifty dollars for ten days of coverage, the cost of one hour of billing by an adequate personal injury attorney.

You will be expected to initial your decision to buy the insurance or not to buy the insurance when you are completing the contract. Your signature will be required, and an imprint of a credit card as well.

If you use a fancy credit card that has accident protection, you may be tempted to skip the insurance. If you have an accident in the car, that credit card will be charged the full value of the vehicle, plus whatever else that they want to charge on it, until the case is settled. So forget about using that credit card for any other purchases for the next six months or the next year or even longer. Also, you will be subject to the judgment of the credit card company and the rental car company as to what you will ultimately owe due to the accident. It might be cheaper in the long run to buy the rental car company insurance.

Others say if you have car insurance on your own car and carry your insurance card, your regular motor vehicle insurance will cover you. But, first you have to make sure your insurance will indeed cover you before you go on your trip, then you have to make sure that you follow their procedures. Different states have different minimum insurance requirements. If there is an accident, there will be a protocol for you to follow. You will be lucky if your auto insurance premiums don't increase the following year.

When you pick up the rental car, make sure you inspect it inside and outside. Make note of any damage to the exterior on the little car diagram that is part of the paperwork you turn in before you leave with your car. Also note any major damage to the interior before you drive away. Without making these notes, you will be held accountable for any damage. You may also want to make sure you know how to use the radio, verify that the heater or air conditioner is working, and check that you are familiar with the location of the wiper and light controls so you won't be figuring it out while you are driving.

When you return the car, return it in the condition in which you received it, or as close as possible. Take any trash out of the car and check the glove box, the door cubbies, and under the seat for any personal belongings. Look in the trunk and backseat before you walk away from the vehicle. Do you have your cell phone, sunglasses, purse, wallet, all your luggage, airline tickets, umbrella, coat, and hats? Allow for enough time to unload the vehicle and go through another inspection with an employee of the company. If during your rental you encountered any mechanical problems with the engine, air conditioner or heater, brakes or other systems, courteously notify the company of the problem. If you do not interface with an employee, then write it on the papers you turn it with the car keys. Without your help they won't know repairs are needed before another customer drives away with the same vehicle.

Focus: When renting a car, read the contract and buy the insurance. Your financial life will be simpler that way.

Day Seven

Personal Responsibility When Driving

When you are driving a car you are operating a lethal weapon.

Yes, you can kill someone with a car, just like you can kill with a knife, a gun, or any other weapon. Keep that in mind when you are running errands, driving on the highway, going to school, slipping off to the mall, or traveling to a friend's house. The tiniest distraction can cause you to lose control of the vehicle and slam over one ton of metal into another car, a person, a bicyclist, a guardrail, a center median, or a motorcyclist, or off an embankment.

You may think you can put on mascara, eat a burger, text your best friend, look up directions to the party, call your sister, sing along to the radio, read a book, slurp on a soda, drive with your knee, write an email, look into the backseat, reach into your purse, yell at your kids, lick a melting ice cream cone, search through your glove box, unwrap a candy bar, look up a phone number, or pet your dog without it affecting your driving, but you are wrong. If you were to kill someone because you were doing one of the above things, how would you feel? Surely it can wait, whatever it is that you think is so important. You wouldn't handle a loaded gun and try to do anything else at the same time, would you?

Stay focused when you drive. Look up directions before you leave. Make and take phone calls only when you are pulled over in a safe place away from traffic. Strap all children into safety seats; consider doing the same for dogs and other pets too. Take advantage of stoplights to have a sip of your soda, check directions, dig through your purse, or adjust the radio. Never text, talk on the phone, write or read an email, or read a book while driving. If you have a reliable passenger, then ask them to be your navigator and communicator to the outside world.

Do not drive if you are under the influence of alcohol or drugs, legal or illegal. Designate a sober driver or hire a cab or driver for a night out on the town. If you must take pain killers or other drugs that affect your motor reflexes, then consider carpooling to work or school or using an alternative method of transportation for the few days you are taking a prescription or while you are healing.

MoneySmarts4U: The Basics

Before you take a trip where you will drive in another state or country, look up the rules of the road online, and review them to make sure you understand what is expected from you while driving elsewhere. Some states may allow right turns on red lights, others may have higher speed limits, and some may limit passing on the highway to the left lane only, with traffic expected to remain in the right lane unless one car is passing another. Don't assume that the laws are the same everywhere, because they are not.

If you are involved in an accident, exchange contact and insurance information with the other parties to the accident. In some jurisdictions parties to an accident are expected to wait for the police for any accident; in others the police are called only if someone is injured. If someone is injured, definitely call for an ambulance and wait for it to arrive.

If you are involved in an accident, write down your recollections of the events that took place immediately, including streets, intersections, weather, light, time of day, and what happened. Take pictures of your vehicle and any other vehicles involved, making sure license tags are included, as well as any damage.   Also take photos of the participants after the fact, in and out of the car. Do your best to maintain your composure even though you may be rattled.

Focus: Be responsible when driving a vehicle. Remember it is a lethal weapon and can kill someone if the operator is negligent or distracted.

Getting Around Town

1. You can save money to spend elsewhere by walking, biking, or taking mass transit.
2. In budgeting for your transportation needs, consider all the expenses including insurance, licensing, and maintenance.
3. If you are going to buy a vehicle, research the features you want, determine the price you are willing to pay, and have a strategy for buying what you want for the price you can afford.
4. Buying a quality used car may give you more features and luxury for your transportation budget.

5. Consider buying a new or used car before leasing a new one.

6. When renting a car, consider buying the insurance from the rental car company. Read the contract before you sign it.

7. Be responsible when driving a vehicle. Do not text, talk on the phone, or play the radio too loud while driving. Remember: it is a lethal weapon, and you can kill someone while driving if you are distracted or negligent.

Week Three: Earning Money

The feeling of being paid for the first time for a job well done is exhilarating. No matter whether the work is mowing the lawn, writing code, washing the dog, creating a painting, filming a movie, or answering the phone, the first link between money and work creates the desire for more of that feeling of satisfaction and accomplishment. Seek out the work that gives you that sense of worthiness, as you will likely spend more time in your life working than doing almost anything else. To look back on your day with a sense of pride at your efforts, whatever they are, is a gift to give yourself.

Day One

Getting Your Foot in the Door

In this day and age of computers and technology, there are a myriad of ways to look for a job. Even though you submit an application online, eventually there will be a face-to-face meeting with someone who will make the decisions about hiring. Who you know may get you the interview, but what you know will get you the job.

Don't be afraid to ask for help finding a job. While you are still in school, ask your teachers, classmates, and the staff at your school, as well as neighbors and local businesses you frequent, about any job opportunities available. Tell them what you are looking for, whether it is part-time work or a full-time job, weekends, nights, holidays, or summers. Start asking four to six months before you really want to start work, but be prepared if there is something available right away.

If you've never had a job aside from the chores you do at home, you may want to volunteer at a local charity to find out how a business is run. Animal shelters, churches or synagogues, soup kitchens, thrift shops, libraries, and other non-profits are businesses that work to serve and benefit others. Working as a volunteer will give you valuable experience keeping a schedule, arriving on time, dressing appropriately for the task at hand, and working with others. You will learn about that particular business, while meeting many contacts that might write recommendations for you or help you find a paying job when you are ready to make that step.

Develop a reputation as a careful and cheerful worker who is always willing to help others. After a while people will be glad to work with you. When there is a job opening where they work, your name will be the first one that pops into their head. They will help you get a job when you need it.

Whenever anyone helps you, whether it is to give you the name of someone to call who might offer you a job or to help you get an appointment for an interview, write him or her a simple snail-mail thank-you note. A handwritten note telling them how grateful you are for their help will stick in their memory because you made the extra effort to write your thoughts on paper, put it in an envelope, and mail it. So few people write thank-you notes that the ones received are memorable.

Focus: Grow your network of friends and acquaintances through your school contacts, neighbors, volunteer work, and cheerful effort. Show your gratitude to those who help you by thanking them graciously with a personal note. Keep them aware of your progress. You will be amazed at how many people truly want to know about you as you develop your life.

Day Two

Before the Interview

If you've made it far enough to get an interview for a position you are interested in, then do some research before you walk in the door. As soon as you know you will be interviewing for a job, start digging for information. Get a head start so that when the day of your interview comes, you are relaxed, confident, and ready.

Research the company you are going to be working for if you want to make a favorable impression. What business are they in? What is their financial situation? Who are their main competitors? What products or services are they known for in the marketplace?

After you research the company, if you know who will be interviewing you, find out what you can about them from online sources, as well as from anyone who may be personally acquainted with your interviewer. Have they been with the company a long time? What is their current title? What are their hobbies? You may feel more comfortable with the process if you know something about the person who will be interviewing you. Remember, everyone goes through a first interview, so take comfort in that as you are asked about your qualifications and your previous experience. An interview works both ways: both you and the interviewer can ask questions. Think of three things you would like to know about the work you would be doing, your role in the company, and your prospects for the future with that company. Asking questions shows that you have an interest in the company and that you care enough to be curious about your role in that business.

Even though you have submitted an application listing your experience and your accomplishments, bring along at least two copies of your resume in case you need it. Some interviewers are overwhelmed with paper, or their computers crash, or they have someone else's information in front of them, not yours, so help them by providing them all the information they need about you.

At least a day before the interview, take the time to drive or travel to the location where you will be meeting the interviewer. Find the building, and if possible the office where you will be going, ahead of time. If you can't physically do this, then make a virtual visit to the location so you have an idea where you will be heading and can approximate the time for traveling to that location. When you are planning your departure for the interview, add an extra twenty to thirty minutes to allow for traffic jams or bad weather.

During the time you are looking for, applying for, and interviewing for a job, put together an interview wardrobe of two to three outfits ahead of time. For each interview be sure the clothing is cleaned and pressed, stain-free, hole-free, and appropriate for the company and position for which you are interested. You want to be remembered for who you are, not what you are wearing.

Focus: Prepare ahead of time for your interview so you can feel confident and make a good impression.

Day Three
The Day of the Interview

Plan your time well the day of an important interview. Allow for extra time in your commute to the location where you will be interviewed. If you can arrive ten to fifteen minutes before your interview appointment, you will have time to relax and mentally review how you would like the interview to go.

Attend to your personal grooming with regular haircuts. Make sure your nails are clean and cut to an appropriate length. Bathe and shampoo the day of the interview. Wear your hair as you normally would. Do not wear excessive amounts of cologne or perfume, as some people are allergic to fragrance. If you wear makeup, be careful to apply just the right amount to accentuate your best features. While you are dressing think positive thoughts about a good outcome to the interview. Remember, in fashion less is more.

When you arrive for your interview, be courteous and pleasant with the receptionist, who is the "gatekeeper." Many times the receptionist's impression of you is valued more heavily than the interviewer's. Be prepared for complications, like the interviewer is running late or they don't have your information or they need you to wait for thirty minutes, all of which may be designed to test your behavior when things go wrong. If you can't accommodate their requests, then explain why and ask to reschedule the interview. Be as courteous as you can. Smile when appropriate. Do not lose your temper or call anyone names. While you are waiting to be seen, make sure all sounds are off on your cell phone or other electronic gadgets.

Once you are called to go in to the interviewer's office, remember to take a deep breath, smile, stand up straight, and walk in confidently with your head high. Shake hands with the interviewer as you introduce yourself. Maintain a pleasant demeanor while you answer any questions they may have, and every once in a while insert your questions. Listen carefully to each question you are asked. Direct questions should not be asked about your age, gender, citizenship, disabilities, family status, credit rating, or military discharge. If you are asked these direct questions, you may wish to respond, "Does this relate directly to my ability to do my job?" And further, "I am confident I will be able to handle the requirements of this position." Keep in mind that if the interviewer persists asking direct questions about these forbidden topics, it may indicate that the workplace will also disregard other aspects of your legal rights.

If you feel the interview is going well, ask about the salary, potential bonuses, benefits, tuition reimbursement (if you want to complete your bachelor's degree or pursue advanced studies), and opportunities for advancement within the company. When the interview is over, remember to thank the interviewer and leave with his or her contact information so you can send them a thank-you email followed by a snail-mail thank-you note.

Focus: Set yourself up for success by being prepared, knowing where you are going, presenting yourself well, acting pleasant, and behaving like someone that YOU would like to work with at that company.

Day Four

When You Are Hired

When you are offered a job, there are a few more hurdles to go through before you are actually an employee. You may need to provide a copy of your Social Security card as well as a form of government-issued identification, usually a driver's license or a passport.

Nowadays most companies require a drug test, fingerprinting, and a complete medical examination, usually paid for by the company hiring you.

In addition, there may be many documents requiring your signature, such as confidentiality agreements and non-compete agreements. Confidentiality agreements usually involve trade secrets or require that clients' names not be discussed outside the firm. Non-compete agreements usually restrict your ability to work in a similar field or with clients you acquire while at that firm. For your future protection, you may want an attorney to review these documents and explain them to you before you sign them.

At some point you will have a meeting with your immediate supervisor or a member of the Human Resources Department who will go over the benefits available to you through the company, like stock purchase plans, retirement plans, insurance plans, sick leave, and vacation days. In addition, you may be subject to a thirty-day, sixty-day, or ninety-day probationary period during which you can be fired without cause. During that period, pay special attention to any criticism, comments, or correction you receive from your immediate supervisor. Keep a private record of these events for your future reference. If there is ever a question about your competence versus a personality dispute with your supervisor, this record could be invaluable if it points to a personal issue rather than a competence issue.

At that same meeting, ask about performance reviews. These are meetings where your supervisor ranks your work performance. Find out how often you will be reviewed and how these reviews will impact your advancement and your salary. Is there a clearly defined career ladder? If you have a negative review, ask whether you can appeal that review, and how that system works. Also, ask whether there is anyone to go to if you feel you are not up to the standards being set and you want to improve in order to keep your job. Unless there is nothing that can be done to help you, most companies want to keep loyal employees.

Focus: Ask questions and pay attention to the process you go through when you are first hired. If you do not understand something you are being asked to sign, have an attorney review it and explain it to you before you do.

Day Five

Your First Paycheck

When you first start out, be aware that most companies pay on a two-week pay period; employees receive a check two times a month, usually on Fridays. If you are in sales, you may have a base pay check that you receive every two weeks, and then an additional bonus check at the end of the month. Keep in mind that whatever salary you are quoted will have items deducted from it, required by law, like Social Security, Medicare, and income tax withholding. These deductions can total up to twenty-one percent or more of your salary earned before you even cash the check.

Depending on the benefits your company offers, other items will be deducted as well, like health insurance, life insurance, disability insurance, stock purchase plan, and retirement plan contributions. If you take advantage of all the benefit opportunities available to you, you may only end up with fifty percent of your base salary available to pay bills and living expenses.

It is important to be able to meet your present obligations, but it is also important to save for later in your life. Before you are married and have children, if that is the lifestyle you choose, you may want to take full advantage of the savings, investment, and retirement plans available to you from your company. Each year you have an enrollment period where you can alter your commitments to these opportunities depending on your life situation. During that enrollment period changes can be made in the amounts withheld to reflect your current status on your life timeline.

Focus: Be aware of when and how much you will be paid. Use fifty percent of your base salary for budgeting purposes. Underestimating your take-home pay will help you provide for yourself and your family in a responsible way for the future.

Day Six

What Do These Benefits Do for Me?

The deductions from your paycheck that are required by law are designed to provide a safety net for U.S. citizens when they are disabled or too old to work. Social Security benefits are paid to people sixty-five years of age and older. Medicare is also for the same age group. The income tax withholding from your check is a pay-as-you-go system to ensure that the government gets its tax money and that you pay your taxes.

Group health insurance that you purchase through your employer may cover you, as well as your spouse and children. The amount you pay goes up based on the number of people covered. The major benefit is that in the event you require medical care or hospitalization, the insurance will cover a portion of that expense. Usually a nominal fee called a co-pay is charged at the time of service, and then the insurance picks up a percentage of the remainder, depending on your deductible. The "deductible" is the portion you pay over a year, over and above the co-pay amount. When the medical services received are greater than the "deductible" portion you pay, then you start to receive your benefits. If you have a large deductible, usually your monthly insurance premium is smaller than when you have a small deductible, which causes your insurance premium to be larger. Either way, the insurance company gets its money, and the doctors and hospitals do too.

Stock purchase plans occur in companies that are publicly traded. Usually on a quarterly basis, the company goes into the marketplace and buys their company stock that they place in the individual accounts of employees participating in the plan. Some companies offer a discount to the market price of anywhere from five percent to fifteen percent of the market price on the day of purchase, thus supplementing the contribution you make by adding an extra five percent to fifteen percent of matching funds. As you accumulate stock over time, the savings can mount up, providing you with another source of funds later on in life for retirement. If the company stock performs well, this is a great way to save money. Companies want their employees to own stock because they are more likely to work harder, vote their stock proxy as management wants, and work toward a common goal of company success.

Retirement plans sponsored by a company that require a contribution on the part of the employee are 401(k) plans for profit-oriented businesses and 403(b) plans for not-for-profit companies. Usually a percentage of each paycheck is deposited into each individual employee's account at each pay period. The money is invested in mutual funds or employee stock. When the annual enrollment period comes around, each employee specifies what funds to invest in and what percentage of their dollars they want in each fund. Make the maximum contribution that is allowed to your 401(k) or 403(b). Over time this money that is working tax-free for you will add up and it will make a big difference in your life later on. If employer stock is the only choice, find out who the plan's trustees are and what obligations they have to the employees. Watch the stock carefully and be sure to diversify your other investments. Yes, this money comes out of your paycheck before you even see it and it will make your take-home amount smaller, but it will be there for you later.

If there are no company retirement plans, then set up an Individual Retirement Account (IRA) and contribute to it each time you get a paycheck, up to the maximum allowed by law. Growing tax free, the money will grow faster than any money you can save and invest after taxes, meaning there won't be tax on the income or appreciation in value of the investments while they are in these tax-deferred accounts. Tax will be paid only when the funds are withdrawn from the account. On Roth IRAs there is no tax on the money as it grows in those accounts, but there are limits to the amount of money you can invest in Roth IRAs.

When you start working for a new company there will be all kinds of new forms to complete related to tax withholding, retirement plans, savings plans, stock purchase plans, and health care options. Ask questions of your supervisor or the Human

Resources officer if you need the forms explained. Understand what you are signing and how your decisions will affect you over the course of your career. Most corporations provide their employees with the opportunities to make changes once a year, usually in the fall prior to the beginning of the New Year.

Focus: Pay yourself first by making contributions to savings through weekly deposits, or direct withdrawals from your paycheck. Take advantage of saving through company-sponsored retirement plans, stock purchase plans, and savings plans. Saving for later in life through stock purchase plans and retirement plans can give you more freedom when you are older. Learn about your investment opportunities and diversify your investment choices.

Day Seven

Working on Your Own

If you have trouble finding a job because of lack of experience, you may want to start your own business. If you are still in school, there may be a need for dog-walkers, house sitters, lawn service, babysitters, tutors, computer assistants, or anything else you can think of that people need and for which people are willing to pay. Starting your own business requires more work on your part in order to market and sell your service or product to others. In addition, you will need to keep track of what you earn, the income tax you owe, any expenses related to your business, and your customer/client base.

Writers and others may freelance, where they sell their work piece by piece to different publications or websites. Some people may run a business out of their home, selling vitamins, cosmetics, or cleaning products; most of these people are paid on commission based purely on what they sell. You may be an artist who designs and sells art, clothing, furniture, or jewelry, works that are unique or custom-made pieces.

Multiplying yourself by creating a product that can be reproduced and sold to many different customers is another way to develop an income stream that can be a vital business. Recording artists, greeting card designers, fashion designers, and software designers are all examples of people who use their talents to multiply their earning potential.

If you choose to enter any of the professions, like law, medicine, accounting, investments, or real estate, you may eventually want to create your own business and either be on your own or create your own company to provide your services the way you want to offer them.

Remember, working for your own personal business has trade-offs. It requires discipline, multiple skills, and flexibility in order to be successful. You may prefer to let someone else take care of the details and work for another's business; on the other hand, you may enjoy the freedom and the challenge of creating your own business.

Focus: Working on your own has its distinct advantages and disadvantages. There is more risk and more responsibility, but also more potential for personal challenge and rewards.

Earning Money

1. Grow your network of friends and acquaintances through your school contacts, neighbors, and volunteer work. Keep them aware of your progress in life.

2. Write personal thank-you notes to people who help you.

3. Prepare ahead of time for your interview by researching the company and the industry.

4. Dress appropriately for the interview. Bring two copies of your resume with you.

5. Read the documents you are required to sign when you are hired. You may want an attorney to review and explain anything you do not understand.

6. When you receive your first paycheck, amounts will be deducted for taxes, Medicare, and Social Security. Additional amounts may be deducted for health insurance, disability insurance, retirement plan contributions, stock purchase plans, and other benefits. Your take-home pay may be fifty percent of the amount quoted to you as your salary.

7. Starting your own business may involve more risk and responsibility, but it does offer a greater potential for rewards as well. Keep track of what you earn, pay your taxes, and maintain a list of your customers.

Week Four: Cash Management Basics

Playing Monopoly as a child, I always wanted to be the banker, even before I could count. I think it was the pretty colors of the different denominations----blue, pink, greens, and yellow----that appealed to me. The first time I served as the banker, I tried to keep all the bills of the same color together and worked to give everyone the right change when they bought any of the properties or hotels during the game.

Recently, I played with some friends whose young sons are sharp and clever, knowing which properties to buy to make the most rents as the game progressed. Making change was the hardest part for them, since they live in a world where everything is purchased with plastic cards. It may take longer to do things by hand or in your head, but eventually, with practice, you'll be able to keep track of numbers and money easier.

As they say in auto racing, in order to win races, you must be able to drive fast without wrecking. To drive fast you must be able to drive slowly. It's the same with money; take it slow at the beginning, even if you have to do it by hand. This will allow you to acquire the skill to manage it faster later on and to manage your money successfully.

Day One
Money In, Money Out

If you wanted candy from a gumball machine when you were little, you asked someone for the money to buy the candy. With small hands you would place that quarter in the slot, turn the knob, and cup your hand carefully to catch the jawbreaker or gumball as it popped out.

As you got older and taller, you could see the cash register at the store where dollar bills, fives, tens, and twenties all lined up in their trays, and pennies, nickels, dimes, and quarters clattered as the clerk made change whenever cash was paid for a purchase. Every denomination was displayed in an orderly fashion. Occasionally you would see one tray of money removed as a checker took a break, while another one replaced it. There was a rhythm to the way the money moved. Money was paid in, money was paid out. Fresh money was brought in, and the accumulated money was taken out.

Learning to take care of your own money has a rhythm to it, too. To know the beat it follows means you have to keep a record of where it comes from and where it goes---money paid in, money paid out, and what if any is left over. Tomorrow, start simple, beginning with a certain amount of cash in your purse or pocket. Make a note of that amount at the top of an index card or on a small piece of paper you keep with you. As you go through the day, only spend cash, and write down the amounts you spend and how you spent it, subtracting from the amount at the top of the card, the amount you started with at the beginning of the day.

For example: You start the day with twenty dollars and then you pay three dollars for parking leaving you with seventeen dollars. Next you have lunch with a friend and spend six dollars, leaving you with eleven dollars. Later, after work you buy a latte for four dollars, leaving you with seven dollars. You discover you are almost out of gasoline and have to stop to buy some, but you only have seven dollars to spend, about enough for two gallons. You are out of money for the day.

The physical, tangible counting out of money can dramatically increase your awareness of where you spend your money and how much you actually spend. To start with, use envelopes labeled for each budget category, such as rent, electric and gas, water, telephone, Internet, groceries, and all the other spending areas. Fill them with the cash amount you budgeted. Write that amount on the front of the envelope, along with the category of spending. Each time you pay for something in that category, subtract that amount from the budgeted figure. Remember, most grocery stores will accept payments for electric and gas, water, Internet, and cable, giving you a receipt in return. Put these receipts in the appropriate envelopes and remember to register them on the appropriate envelope. At the end of the month, notice whether you have any money left over and, if so, where it is. Did you "borrow" from one of the other categories? How did that feel? Taking payments to the actual businesses or their surrogate may take extra time, but remember this is a learning experience to ingrain in your mind the actual feeling of spending the money and the awareness of where your money is going once you earn it.

Focus: By actually handling the cash due for your expenses, you have a physical memory of the transaction as well as a chance to stop and ask yourself if you want to make that purchase or spend that money. This method gives you a new habit of awareness of how you choose to spend your money. Registering your expenditures by hand will also reinforce the awareness of what you are doing with your money.

Day Two

Checking Accounts

Although you can pay cash for food, clothes, shoes, gas, and many other things, there is a point where carrying too much cash is risky. Who knows when your purse or wallet might be stolen? You may want to consider opening a bank account, but know that if you deposit ten thousand dollars or more in cash at one time at a bank, there are reporting requirements to be complied with by the bank and by you. Once you open a bank account, you may choose to make withdrawals by writing checks, using a debit card, or making electronic transfers in order to pay bills or make purchases.

A woman who opened an account at her local bank was thrilled when she received a box of five hundred checks right after she opened her account. She merrily wrote checks for everything under the sun; her rent, a new dress, a car payment, groceries, and a new necklace. A week later she was notified that her account was overdrawn. When she called the bank, she said, "I don't understand why there is a problem. You sent me all these checks. I thought as long as I had checks I had money in my bank account."

Bank accounts that offer checking privileges as well as debit cards allow a defined number of checks to clear each month, as well as a limited number of debit card transactions. Be careful when you use checks, as they have your bank account number on them and are often used by identity thieves to capture that information as well as your signature. When you use debit cards or credit cards to purchase items online, make sure the URL of the webpage begins with https and the security lock icon is visible before entering your card information.

In the check register that comes with your account, make a note of the check number, to whom it was written, and the amount, then subtract it from the balance of your opening deposit. Use the register to note transactions with your debit card as well, noting the day, amount, and where you used it, and subtract the expense from your balance. When you make a deposit into your account, add it to your balance, noting the date, the source, and the amount. Use your register to note where your money comes from and where your money goes.

When you write a check you date it, then fill in the name of the person or business you are paying. You follow that up with writing the amount using numbers, for example $25.00, in the space provided next to the Payee blank. Then below that line, write out the amount using words, in this case, "twenty-five dollars and 00/100 cents," to reinforce the correct figure to be paid. In the memorandum space, at the bottom left of the check, write the invoice number or bill number or purpose of the check----example, Rent for June or Account Ending in 2556. Finally sign your name, in the blank at the bottom right of the check. Your signature should match that on the signature page of the bank account application. Maybe you sign only your first and last name or include your middle name, or middle initial, or maybe you have a swooshy signature, but whatever it is make sure you can consistently repeat it every time you sign your checks.

Be sure you know how many checks you can write a month on your account before you begin paying your bills. When your bills come in, a due date will be posted on the front of the bill. Order your bills by due date, with the ones due soonest first, and the later ones at the back. If you are going to mail your payment in, then allow a week to ten days for mail service, paying your bills in advance of the due date. To make things easier for you and to keep you organized, pay all your bills on the same day of the week, and if possible write all the checks at the same time.

Establishing a regular time and day to sit down to pay bills allows you to get in the habit of tending to your money and keeping your financial data organized. File your bills by category: water and sewer, electric, Internet, and so on. As you are paying your bills, note the amount of each one on your budget sheet under "actual," then calculate the difference for the month from your budgeted amount. Note each check and subtract the amount from the balance. When your bank statement comes in, then balance your checkbook, as instructed on the back of the statement. Mail the bills ten days in advance of the due date to be assured that they will arrive in a timely fashion. If while paying bills by check, using a check register to note each expenditure, you are still over budget at the end of the month, then you may need to use only cash for a few months until you figure out where you are spending too much or if you need additional income from another job.

When you write checks from your bank account, remember the money is taken out of your account, so keep track of your balance to avoid being overdrawn.

Focus: When you use checks to pay bills, keep track of your balance by using the register and your monthly statements, and balancing your account every month.

Day Three
What Are Debit Cards?

A young man established a checking account where he signed up for a debit card. This card looked like a credit card, but it was a debit card: the money he spent was immediately subtracted or removed from his checking account. He kept having overdrafts in his account and was charged overdraft fees, but also fees related to the overuse of his debit card. No one explained to him how the card worked, because he did not ask the issuer about the features of the account and the card issued to him. Once it was explained to him that every time he used the card the money came out of his account, he understood why he was charged overdraft and overuse fees, as well as bounced check charges.

Debit cards linked to your checking, savings, or securities account take the money out of the account when you withdraw cash at an ATM (automatic teller machine) or use the debit card to purchase items like gas, clothing, groceries, and any other merchandise. Keeping track of your account balance and replenishing the account when it reaches a minimum balance is your responsibility. Using a check register to note purchases, or retaining the receipts to note those expenses on your budget sheet, are good habits to acquire. Some debit cards can only be used to take cash from an ATM. Others can be used almost everywhere to make purchases. Some may have limits as to the amount used on a daily basis or on the number of times the card is used each day; others may limit expenditures to whatever balance is in the account. If your debit card is stolen, it could expose you to losing the entire balance in your account, so report a theft of the card or any identity theft problems you may have to the issuing institution as soon as you know. Some institutions have insurance to cover unauthorized transactions by unauthorized users.

Another kind of debit card is a prepaid card. The amount of money loaded onto the card is the maximum limit for expenditures until the card is once again reloaded with funds. If a card has one thousand dollars loaded onto it, then up to one thousand dollars can be spent with that card, until it is replenished with more money. If the card is lost, only the remaining balance on the card is vulnerable to theft. If your identity is stolen, then all that is accessible to the thief is the remaining balance on the card. A fee may be required to purchase, refill, use, or maintain the card. Ask the issuer about these fees and read the materials provided before you choose a prepaid card.

If you only want to spend the money you have and do not want to take on consumer debt with a credit card, then using a debit card may be a good idea for you. After you have kept your budget figures by hand long enough to know how you are spending your money, then you may want to take advantage of banking and accounting software that links to your account and automatically categorizes your spending based on where you spend your money, making it easy to maintain your budget and expense plan. Ask your banker about this kind of accounting software that links to their system. Keeping an eye on your balance as well as your spending in various categories will help you accomplish your financial goals.

Prepaid cards can be helpful if you are working to limit your expenditures to a certain amount each month. By loading that amount on a prepaid card you will be forced to stop spending when you "run out" of money on the card. Much like having a limited amount of cash in your pocket to spend during the month, a prepaid card can help you maintain spending limits.

Focus: Debit cards, both prepaid cards and those linked to an account, can give you the ease of electronic money but also help you limit your expenses to the money you actually saved and have available to spend. Living within your means will help you achieve your life goals, allowing you to save money for the lifestyle you want to live.

Day Four
Pay Yourself First
Start Building Your Nest Egg and
Emergency Fund

Learning to save is one of the most important skills you can develop. What is your inspiration for saving? Having the money you need when you need it. So many times we hear the phrase "Save for a rainy day." Not knowing when you will have an emergency or a tear in your financial umbrella is the same as not knowing when it is going to rain: hard to predict but still a possibility that requires planning.

Start with accumulating a nest egg of one thousand dollars as your first step in your savings plan. How to do that? If you set aside three dollars a day for a year you would save one thousand ninety-five dollars. Putting twenty dollars in the bank once a week for a year saves one thousand forty dollars. Give up fancy coffee drinks. Take your lunch to work or school. Take the bus or walk instead of driving and parking. Have movie night at home instead of going out. Look for small ways to build up this first emergency fund. In one year you could accomplish your first financial goal of saving one thousand dollars.

Now that you've saved one thousand dollars for your nest egg, it's time to work on saving six to nine months worth of expenses. To prepare for any long-term emergency, like losing your job or experiencing a pay cut, demotion, or medical emergency, building up six to nine months worth of expenses in a savings account or interest-bearing checking account is a good plan.

Although no one likes to face any kind of disappointment in their professional life, having funds set aside for just such an event makes it easier to move forward with your life. Take the total amount you want to save and divide by fifty weeks to figure out how much you will have to pay yourself to save up that amount in reserve. Yes, you may have to forget buying that drink at the coffee shop, or take your lunch to school or work, but imagine how good you will feel when you've saved up enough money to take care of yourself in the event you lose your job or need time off to look for another one.

Your nest egg and emergency fund belong in an insured interest-bearing checking or savings account permitting ready access to the money in an emergency. An insured CD with no penalty for early withdrawal is another option for this money.

Focus: Preparing for an emergency by saving money a little bit at a time is a responsible, loving thing to do for yourself.

Day Five

Creating Your Spending Plan

How can you know how much money you need to save? Draft a spending plan, also known as a budget. Make a list of your monthly expenses, item by item. Gather all your bills together from last month. Write down the category: rent/mortgage, electric bill, water bill, groceries, prescriptions, health insurance, personal care, gasoline, car payment, car maintenance, entertainment, and so on. A detailed worksheet is found at the end of this reading. Each month, as your bills come in, make a note of the expenses by category. When estimating how much to save, you can multiply your first month by six or by nine in order to guesstimate the number that is your savings goal.

Often this exercise reveals that you are spending more than you make, giving you a chance to make minor adjustments to your spending habits. Adjusting your spending to address your needs as opposed to your wants may make it easier for you to save money.

Pay attention to how and when you spend your money. Do you spend more money when you are sad? Angry? Lonely? Happy? Jealous? Envious? Becoming aware of your spending habits and the emotions that accompany them can make a major difference in your financial and emotional well-being.

Living with a spending and savings plan is a flexible experience. Build a few treats into your spending plan. Create a vacation fund or a date night fund to enhance the life of your relationship. Just like with being on a diet, there will be times you will be tempted to "cheat" on your savings plan. Making spending decisions involves weighing the cost of one thing compared to another, often referred to as opportunity cost. When you spend money on a new electronic gadget, you give up the opportunity to spend that money on the down payment on a new car. If you buy the latest fashion, in style for a few months, you give up the opportunity to purchase a classic handbag or pair of fabulous shoes later on.

Luxury can be had for free or at a discount, but you have to look for it. Consignment shops in the more affluent parts of town may feature gently worn designer clothes and accessories at deeply discounted prices. When shopping for everyday necessities, peruse the coupon rack at the grocery store and look at the advertising circulars in the newspaper. Search the websites of brand name products and prescription medications for coupons. Local television or radio stations may offer discounts for restaurants and movies. There are also websites dedicated to nothing but coupons for all sorts of savings opportunities.

Last minute walk-up customers can often purchase discounted tickets at the box office for theatrical performances or sporting events. Most museums offer visitors free admission one evening or one day each week. Live theater and movies may be seen for free at local parks or botanical gardens. Membership contributions to civic organizations like museums, zoos, and public radio or television can include free or discounted tickets for cultural events. Take advantage of the free entertainment opportunities in your locale.

If material goods are not your spending vice, then maybe you want to take a trip to Paris, leading you to forgo your daily latte or restaurant meals for a time in order to save the money you need for the travel experience of your dreams. Awareness of the opportunity costs of your everyday lifestyle can lead you to a more balanced life where the mental, physical, emotional, and spiritual work in harmony to help you develop habits that benefit you throughout your life.

Focus: A spending and savings plan that reflects your needs over your wants can bring about habits that lead to a balance of the mental, physical, emotional, and spiritual parts of your life.

Barbie's Budget Worksheet

Category	Budget	Actual	Difference
Savings ($1000)			
Savings (6-9 months)			
Savings (Retirement)			
Rent			
Electric & Gas			
Phone			
Internet/Cable/TV			
Health Insurance			
Grocery			
Car Payment or Transportation			
Car Insurance			
Home Insurance			
Grooming			
Clothing			
Charitable Gifts			
Entertainment and Travel			
Maintenance and Replacement			
Total:			

Day Six

Keeping Track of Your Money

When I was a little girl, about six years old, my parents paid me to do chores around the house. There were coffee tables to wipe down, trashcans to empty, and ashtrays to clean. Later, when I was older, I washed cars and vacuumed and maintained the swimming pool, in addition to my other chores. I was paid at the end of each week, based on how many days of the week I did my work. I put half my money in a piggy bank to save for Christmas gifts for family and close friends. The rest of the money I spent as I pleased, for candy, toys, puzzles, ice cream, and other indulgences. If I missed a day of chores, I did not get paid. I learned to equate work and money. I also apply that same strategy to the money I earn today, with half of it going into savings and the rest applied to everyday expenditures, taxes, and indulgences.

Living beyond one's means is a real problem for a lot of people these days simply because they want more than they need. There is so much media stimulation telling people that the latest car, the best clothes, new furniture, and eating out will make them happy. Peer pressure complicates matters, especially when you are just out of school and don't have much income. It is important to know what makes you happy and what satisfies you. I'm not saying don't aspire to own nice things, but do so over time, saving money along the way until you can pay for it and wait until you have an income that supports the lifestyle you choose.

Some people need to experience a physical representation of what they spend and how they spend their money. With all the electronic means of spending available today---credit cards, debit cards, phone swiping, wands, scanners, and finger swiping---it is easy to electronically empty your bank account without any awareness of where your money goes.

A spending plan, or budget, can help you see where your money has to go and where you want it to go. Your monthly bills will help you figure out what your living costs are and how much discretionary money you have left over, if any, for frills, like new clothes, entertainment, or eating out. If you find you are "out of money" at the end of the month, then it might be time to return to a tangible spending plan until you automatically acknowledge where you do and do not want your money to go.

When I was staying with my aunt one weekend, she showed me a spiral notebook in which she wrote down all the expenditures she made as a newlywed. Her husband was in college right after World War II, and they were living in a small apartment near campus with very little income, so she was expected to economize and carefully spend and save their money. As I looked down the page, I saw records written in pencil in her elegant handwriting, entries for "one can pork and beans fifteen cents," "one loaf bread twenty cents," and the like, with a running total of expenditures and a remaining balance. My aunt and uncle knew where every dollar he made was spent. When he retired they had a beautiful home, three married children with families of their own, a well-funded retirement account, and educational trusts for all of their grandchildren. Every year they took a two-week vacation. Their marriage lasted over fifty years. Spending your money carefully can make you as much money as investing your money wisely.

As your life becomes more complicated, you will have more money to manage. You will advance from cash to checks to debit cards to credit cards to electronic transfers. You will go from having cash, to a bank checking account, to an investment account, to a retirement account, to multiple accounts of various kinds. Somehow you will need to keep track of your money. You can't stuff it under the mattress or bury it in the backyard. You can't keep it all in one bank account, so you need to learn about how to take care of it in a way that makes sense for you and your life.

Use whatever works for you to keep track of your money. If writing your accounts in a spiral notebook by hand gives you the sense of where your money is coming from and going to, then use it. If you prefer a spreadsheet on your computer, then design one that is perfect for your needs. Commercially available programs like Quicken are easy to set up and simple to learn. Mobile programs available for your smart phones allow you to enter data as you spend your money, and this way you can see instantly where you stand with your spending plan. Some financial institutions have links to proprietary software that can make keeping track of your money a breeze.

Focus: Creating order in your world of money will require you to keep records of where your money comes from and where it goes. Use the system that works for you.

Day Seven

Save for What You Want

Every time there has been a financial crisis in the United States, spending beyond our means and taking on debt, individually, as businesses or as a country, contributed to the problem. When is taking on debt a sound financial idea? If you are buying something that lasts, like a house, or if you are buying something that produces income sufficient to pay off the debt; these are appropriate transactions where debt makes financial sense. Remember when you are making calculations to be pessimistic in your projections of income produced or market value increases. When you evaluate your purchase, don't assume that you will get a raise or that you will see a consistent income stream. Be conservative with your estimates.

Anything that is worth less due to depreciation after you purchase it, like a new car or new boat or any product with a markup, is best paid for outright, without financing the purchase. Save money for what you want. Don't buy it on credit or finance it over time. Clothes, makeup, shoes, purses, furniture, appliances, electronic gadgets, and many other items will end up costing you more if you finance them over time because you will pay the purchase price plus the interest charged on the purchase price. Meanwhile the value of your purchase depreciates or gets used up over time.

Another advantage of saving money for what you want is that it gives you time to decide whether you really want that particular item. It protects you from casual spending when you may not be making a well-thought-out choice about how you are spending your money. It allows you to savor your decision and enjoy the pleasure of your purchase, rather than buying something without thinking and later regretting your choice.

Focus: If you want something, save money for it, and then buy it if you still want it. Take pride in owning a car, furniture, a boat, or whatever you select when you have the money to pay for it.

Cash Management

1. Consider learning about money through using cash to pay your bills.

2. Pay your bills at the same time and on the same day of the week. File your bills by category.

3. Register purchases and expenses in the "Actual" column of your budget worksheet.

4. Write checks, register those expenditures, balance your checkbook and maintain your budget.

5. If you cannot make ends meet, use the envelope system for several months to reveal your spending issues.

6. When using debit cards, consider using software linked to your bank account to track and organize your spending information to facilitate adhering to your budget.

7. Read about and learn how your bank account, checks, and debit card work.

8. Debit cards used properly can help you live within your means and limit your expenditures.

9. Start saving money for your nest egg of one thousand dollars and your emergency fund of six to nine months worth of expenses. Divide what you want to save by fifty weeks to figure out how much to set aside each week.

10. Look for discounts, coupons, and memberships that give you a luxury experience for less.

11. Create a budget or spending plan.

12. Find a way to keep track of your money that works for you.

13. Save money to buy what you really want.

Week Five: Credit and Debt Management

Throughout your life you may find that you need to take on debt or utilize credit----in other words, borrow money. Sometimes it may be a casual loan from a friend to pay for your lunch because you left your wallet at home. At other times it may be to purchase something expensive like a car or a place to live. A loan is a contractual obligation where one party provides money to another party with the understanding that the money will be paid back, along with an additional amount charged for the use of the money, called interest. The term of the loan is the time the loan is in existence and specifies over what period the interest payable is calculated. Interest can be calculated on an annually, quarterly, monthly, or daily basis. Compound interest refers to the practice of adding the interest charged back to the principal so that there is then interest charged or earned on the interest as well. The annual percentage rate, or APR, is the rate calculated to notify consumers of the effective rate of interest over a year when the compounding period is less than one year. Other forms of loans are credit cards, charge accounts, car loans, mortgage loans, student loans, margin loans, personal loans, and non-recourse loans.

Day One
Credit Cards and Charge Accounts

Using credit and debt appropriately will make your life better in the long run. Wait until you have saved your nest egg of one thousand dollars and created your six-to-nine-month emergency fund before you consider applying for a credit card. Resolve that you will pay the credit card bill in full each month when you receive the bill; otherwise, don't bother to apply for a card.

Using a credit card is like taking out a sort of loan. A credit card issued by a financial institution allows you to make purchases without being directly linked to a savings, checking, or investment account. It is secured by your personal promise to pay off the money you borrow when you use the card for purchases. When you apply for a credit card or charge account, you sign an application form that is a contract specifying the terms of the loan. It will spell out when the payments need to be made and when interest rates begin to apply. If you do not pay the amount due in full, then interest charges will apply on the balance, with rates that can range from five percent to twenty-five percent compounding on a daily basis. At an interest rate of twenty-five percent it only takes 2.88 years for the balance due to double if it is not paid back in full.

When a card is issued to you, there is a maximum limit set for the total amount you may charge at any one time on the card. "Maxing out" your card means charging or spending the maximum limit allowed on the card. Do not "max out" your credit cards, as this will adversely affect your credit score.

Pay in full the amount due on the card so that the money is received before the due date for the payment. Usually cards expect payment each month if a balance is due on the account. If you cannot pay the full amount on the card in any given month, then pay the minimum amount due on time, take the card out of your wallet or purse, discontinue using it, and do not use it again until you have paid off the entire balance.

Credit cards make money for banks, other financial institutions, and stores when you don't pay the amount due in full. They charge you interest at an exorbitant amount, usually anywhere from five percent to twenty-five percent or more on the unpaid balance. Nonpayment sets you up to owe at least double or triple the amount you borrowed on the credit card, if not more.

When a store offers you a discount off your purchase if you apply for a credit card with their store, it may sound like a good deal, but they are not doing you any favors. Impulsively applying for a credit card does not give you time to read and understand the terms of the credit agreement or to verify the interest rate to be charged. The store hopes they will earn more than the discounted amount if you do not pay the amount due in full in a timely fashion. Avoid store-specific credit cards offering discounts on first purchases.

When a credit company offers you points to use their card, remember you have to pay in full each month or you will not be rewarded the points. Evaluate whether the points and the benefits you receive are worth the membership fees you pay to use the card. Don't let status, the offer of something free, some reward, or some other prize convince you that you must have that credit card.

If you find that you are unable to pay the amount due in full, then put the card away in a safe place where you cannot use it. Consider freezing it in a glass of water so that you would have to thaw it out in order to use it. If that doesn't work, then cut the card up into tiny pieces and throw it away.

If you find that you are an impulsive shopper with your credit card, study your purchases and the mood you were in at the time you made them. Happy? Try dancing instead. Sad? Have a good cry. Write in a journal about your feelings and how you feel when you shop. When you feel that way again, then stop and think about what you are doing to yourself. Learn to delay purchases until you can pay for them in full.

If you are an online shopper, confine yourself to a specific time to shop and only for one hour at a time. Never shop online after you have been drinking alcohol. If you are under the influence of drugs that affect your mental acuity, do not buy anything on the Internet. Refrain from using computers, smart phones, or tablets when under the influence. Making a purchase with your credit card, whether online, on the phone, or in person, is a contract whereby you agree to pay the amount specified in exchange for the item or service involved. Part of making a contract is being of sound mind at the time you make it. Keep your part of the agreement.

If for some reason you have any other consumer debt, such as private credit accounts with individual merchants, pay those debts off as quickly as possible. Owing any money to others makes you indebted to another until you pay the amount off. Pay your debt off and be free of obligations to others.

Focus: Apply for credit cards only when you can fully pay the debt incurred when using one. The best time to apply for a credit card is when you don't need one.

Day Two

Payday Loans

Beware of "payday loans" that charge a flat fee per one hundred dollars loaned for a short, perhaps two-week period of time, along with interest, the total due usually coinciding with the borrower's next payday. This fee is often limited in some jurisdictions to fifteen dollars per one hundred dollars loaned. The calculated APR on these types of loans is close to three thousand five hundred percent per year. Lenders are paid back with a postdated check drafted by the borrower on their checking account, or through an electronic transfer. If the borrower has insufficient funds in their account when the check clears or the transfer is made, then there are additional overdraft and banking fees that have to be paid off as well. Obviously, this is a high-risk way to borrow money, with a ridiculously high rate of interest, but the real danger is the tendency to get behind in all your financial obligations as you service this debt or become addicted to using these types of loans as a stopgap solution to your financial problems. Better to draft an expense plan and follow it than spend your money on high amounts of interest.

Focus: Use your budget and your bill cycle to map out a plan to pay your bills on time without having to take out a very expensive payday loan.

Day Three
Student Loan Debt

More and more young adults are finding themselves saddled with more student loan debt than they can pay off over their lifetimes. Before you consider taking on student loan debt, look at the alternative ways you can pay for college and skill certification courses on your own. Working several jobs, taking fewer hours over a longer number of years, attending online courses for less expensive degrees, making private loan agreements with private individuals: all of these are ways that students are getting their advanced education without being saddled with thousands of dollars of debt. It may take you ten years to get your degree, but when you do, you will be free of debt. Look into different kinds of scholarships and see whether you qualify. Find out if your employer has a tuition reimbursement program that you can participate in while you work full-time and go to school part-time. Many entry-level positions will pave the way for hard-working, loyal employees to work their way up the ladder at work and pay for a portion of their school tuition as well.

Don't get your heart set on going to a particular school, especially private schools that actually make money on the student loans they provide to their pupils. Consider starting at an area community college for your core coursework, making sure that the credits transfer to a four-year university. With the crisis related to student loan debt, many universities are offering affordable four-year degrees through online courses.

Before you begin a course of study, visit with the placement office at your school that works with companies who are looking for new hires, and find out what the employment record is for different majors and what the entry-level salary ranges are. Look at the U.S. Labor Department website, www.mynextmove.org, for additional information about career opportunities and salary levels. You may decide to change your major to one where you can easily be employed on graduation, while you minor in the area that you are most interested but may not have great work opportunities. Millions of people return to school to acquire advanced degrees or to study the esoteric subject matter of their dreams while they work in an area where they are well paid.

Focus: Avoid student debt if possible by paying as you go, utilizing alternative educational opportunities, and looking for scholarships or work-study programs that may suit your needs.

Day Four

Car Loans and Mortgages

Car loans usually have terms of three to five years, since that is the depreciable life of an automobile. Depending on your credit score and other factors, interest rates on car loans can range from three percent to twenty-five percent or more. Car payments are usually payable monthly and include interest and principal payments, so that by the end of the loan term the car is fully paid off. The resale value of the car is the collateral or backing for the loan. If you miss too many payments or stop paying altogether, the loan company will repossess the car, causing you to lose all the money you previously paid, as well as the car.

Mortgage loans are long-term loans from three years to thirty years offered to homebuyers to facilitate the purchase of a house, condominium, or townhouse. Interest rates historically have ranged from 3.53 percent to 17.48 percent for thirty-year loans. Usually anywhere from ten percent to twenty percent of the total purchase price is required as a down payment, with the remainder eligible to be borrowed in the form of a mortgage. If you want to purchase a house for $100,000, and want to finance it, you will need to pay a $10,000 to $20,000 down payment from your savings, and then obtain a mortgage, collateralized by the house and land, for the remaining $90,000 to $80,000. The down payment is a portion of the "equity" in your home. Normally each monthly payment includes both principal and interest, and the principal payment increases the equity you have in your home. If during the course of the loan the market value of the house drops below the remaining loan amount, then it is considered that you are "upside down" or "underwater" with your loan, owing more money than the house is worth in the marketplace. If you miss too many payments or stop paying altogether, then your home will be foreclosed on and you will be evicted from your house.

Fiscal conservatives believe it is best to borrow money only when purchasing items of lasting value. For the most part, the only loan obligation one should take on is a mortgage on the house one calls a home.

Focus: Borrowing money comes with the obligation to pay it back. Not doing so can affect your reputation, your future opportunities, and your ability to effectively accomplish life goals that are meaningful to you. Before borrowing money, make sure that you can pay it back and that the purpose for the loan is valid for you and your values.

Day Five

Credit Scores—Your FICO Score

When consumer credit cards were introduced decades ago, the relationship with your banker determined your accessibility to credit. Now the interest rate you pay and the amount of money you can borrow are determined by a mathematical calculation that produces a number called a credit score, known as your FICO score.

Various factors are utilized in determining your FICO score, including your profession, your income, where you live, how much debt you already have, your previous record for paying off debt, the number of credit cards you have and the credit limits on those cards, and the balances you have in investment, savings, and bank accounts, as well as other factors.

Once a year take a look at your credit report to see what it says. You can request a free copy of your report once a year from each of the following credit rating agencies: Equifax will provide you your BEACON score, Experian will provide you the Experian/Fair Isaac Risk Model (FICO), and Transunion will give you the EMPIRICA score. If you disagree with any of the information on the report, write a letter explaining the error and ask to have it corrected. It is up to you to monitor and validate your credit score and the information posted in the report that affects it. Do not pay a credit counseling service to remove "accurate" information from your report, as it results in an expense to you and cannot be legally done. Please be aware that the website FreeCreditReport.com does NOT actually give you a report for free.

FICO scores range from 300 to 850, with 300 being the lowest or worst score, and 850 being the highest or best score. A low FICO score indicates that the consumer has a greater risk of not paying back loans. It also indicates that the consumer may have trouble managing credit. A high FICO score indicates that the consumer has a higher likelihood of paying back loans and that they have managed credit well.

Focus: You are responsible for managing your money well, and that includes managing credit well. One way to manage credit well is to annually review credit reports to ensure they accurately reflect your ability to manage credit.

Day Six
Why Do Credit Scores and Reports Matter?

When you look for a job or apply for a credit card, a car loan, or a mortgage, your credit score will be a factor in whether you get the job, are issued a credit card, or receive the financing you requested to buy a car or a home. Lots of other information, including copies of other loans or obligations you may have, copies of statements of investment and bank accounts you have, documentation of your income earned and your future income potential, will come into play when you want to borrow money for that milestone event in your life. Your credit scores are objective evaluative tools of the financial industry that reflects your ability to manage credit and pay off loans. By managing credit well, paying off credit cards on time, having very little debt compared to your income, and taking care of your financial obligations, you will maintain a credit score that qualifies you for a lower interest rate and the loan amount you requested.

Focus: Your credit score is representative of your money management skills. Being a good steward of your financial assets will enable you to work toward your personal life goals with less stress and less expense, thereby reaping the rewards of your careful choices and planning.

Day Seven

Building and Enhancing Your Credit Score

What improves your credit score is the careful management of credit. It is easier to build or manage credit if you do so slowly. Apply for one credit card at a time. Do not apply for multiple cards in a short period of time in order to increase the amount of credit available to you.

If you are shopping for rates on car loans, credit cards, or mortgages, do so within a finite period of time of fourteen days. If you are applying for a mortgage to buy or refinance a house, applying for new credit cards, car loans, or changing employers will work against you.

If you have other debt, like a car loan or a mortgage, pay it on time as well. Any utility bills, water bills, or rent should be paid on or before the due date. Any entity that lets you use services must be paid in a timely fashion to avert a bad report to a credit agency.

Focus: Pay off all credit card balances in full every month. Pay all your bills on or before the due date. Stop using your credit cards if you are unable to make the full payment due. Managing your credit wisely will enhance and build your credit score.

Credit and Debt Management

1. Read and understand the credit agreement before you apply for a credit card.
2. Apply for a credit card only after you have saved your nest egg and emergency fund.
3. Pay off your credit card bill in full each month. If you are unable to do so, discontinue using the card.
4. Keep track of your credit, debit, ID cards, and passport. Keep them in a safe place when they are not in use.
5. Pay all your bills so the money owed is received on or before the due date. If you are unable to do so, contact the entity and discuss an alternative payment plan to remain in effect until you can fully pay your bills.

6. Avoid payday loans.

7. Rather than take on student loan debt, consider alternatives like community college courses, online programs, alternative certification programs, work-study, or part-time student opportunities.

8. Learn to manage credit well by being a good steward of your money.

9. Get a free copy of your credit report annually from any of the three agencies that track that information: Equifax, Experian, and Transunion.

10. Use debt to purchase items of lasting value, like a house you can live in.

Week Six: Legal and Financial Matters

Legal documents and contracts are involved in every facet of your life. Learning to "read the rulebook" is one of the most important things you can do to take care of yourself financially. When I ran an Indy Car team, the rulebook was the bible for what you could and could not do. The rulebook can be a credit card application, a power of attorney, a non-compete agreement: it can be any contract you sign or agree to that affects your work, your recreational activities, your lifestyle.

Day One
Read and Understand Everything You Sign

One day a man came into my office at the firm where I worked to set up an account for his wife. I gave him the forms, explaining that she needed to sign the new account documents and the transfer forms as well as provide a statement showing the assets she wanted to transfer to her new account. The account was set up and the assets transferred in. About a month later, he came in with a letter, signed by his wife, on her letterhead, transferring all of the assets in her account to a joint account in both their names, on which either of them could write checks. Shortly afterward, an attorney contacted me to inquire about this transfer, whether it was done properly with a letter of transfer, and asked to see the documents setting up the joint account, as well as the letter. Fortunately for me, the signatures were valid and they matched up. All the paperwork required was in order, but it was unfortunate for the female client. Apparently her husband, who had been married five times before, was wanted in five other states for forgery and theft from his previous wives.

The one technique he used in all the cases was to ask them to sign a group of documents, one of which was a blank sheet of their own stationery or a blank sheet of paper. He piled one document on top of the others, never letting his wives read or look at each document before it was signed. Had they read and understood what they were signing, those women would still have the millions of dollars he stole from them. Read and understand anything before you sign it.

Until you reach legal age, which in most states is eighteen years of age, you really aren't held accountable for your actions. You can't have an email account, a charge account, or a securities account or operate a vehicle or swipe a credit card, unless your parents set it up for you and take responsibility for your actions. However, once you turn eighteen, the world looks at you as a full-fledged adult and starts throwing you offers of credit accounts, automobile sales, investment accounts, insurance offers, tenant agreements; all sorts of applications are sent your way. These applications are considered contracts, a mutually binding agreement between two or more parties, enforceable against any party for non-performance. Non-performance can mean non-payment or non-compliance or any number of things usually specified in the contract itself.

Learn to read the fine print. Before you even consider renting an apartment, setting up a utility account, buying a car, getting a credit card, or any other dollar-spending activity, request or pick up applications, blank ones, and read them. Yes, they are the most boring reading in the world. The terminology is intentionally complicated, the language arcane, and the pacing slow. However, the more you read these documents the better you get at recognizing the rhythm and the composition of these contracts. Most of the time they are composed of "boilerplate" language that is common in most contracts. If you do not understand what you are being asked to sign, or if the terms of the document are not agreeable to you or are not reasonable to you, then DO NOT SIGN IT.

I recently purchased an automobile, paying cash for it. One of the documents the dealership wanted me to sign was a credit application. I didn't need credit. I didn't need to have my credit score affected by a credit application from an auto dealer. I refused to sign it. In fact, I told them that if signing that document was a requirement for the transaction, then I didn't want to buy the car. They didn't make me sign the form. I bought the car.

What was going on there? How to lie with statistics: the dealership wanted to pad the numbers of credit applicants for the credit arm of the manufacturer. It was all about them, not at all about what was best for me, the customer. "Let the buyer beware," or caveat emptor is a useful phrase. Don't let the friendly salespeople fool you—they just want to make a sale, and if you are not carefully reading and understanding what you sign, you will set yourself up for some disappointments and major headaches.

Focus: Read and understand everything you sign. If it is unreasonable or not applicable in your situation, refuse to sign it and walk away from the transaction.

Day Two
Monitoring Your Savings and Investments

Every financial institution sends you a statement electronically or by snail mail quarterly or monthly. File these statements together in a notebook or save them electronically to compare each new month to the month before it. Read your statements carefully. Verify that you made the withdrawals that are shown. Are the amounts correct? Is the vendor one you remember doing business with? Record electronic transactions, as well as any checks you write in your check register, to allow you to cross-reference your purchases and deposits. Make sure everything is correct. Most financial institutions only give you thirty days to notify them if there is an error, after which you have no recourse.

If you have investments more sophisticated than a checking or savings account, review the securities in your portfolio for maturities or dividends requiring reinvestment. Are all your stock shares represented on the statement? If there is an inexplicable change or an unfamiliar transaction, then contact your financial firm and make an inquiry. Note the date, the time, and the person with whom you spoke and summarize your conversation on the statement in question or on your calendar. If you are not satisfied with the explanation given, then ask to be transferred to a supervisor----again, making notes along the way.

MoneySmarts4U: The Basics

Keeping scrupulous records will protect you from rogue brokers, Internet hackers, and other nefarious schemes designed to separate you from your money. Making the assumption that you don't have to review your statements and verify transactions is very dangerous. Work in partnership with your investment professional or learn to do it yourself. Learn the tax laws that apply to investment gains and losses to take the most money off the table when it is time for profit taking.

In downturns in the market, be wary of reacting too hastily because of your fears of losing money. Hopefully you will have been taking profits over the years, accumulating some cash to invest in a market downturn, buying stocks or bonds you are interested in at lower prices than available before. Maintain a list of companies you are interested in purchasing and at what price ranges. Also, have a target price for companies you already own to sell for a profit.

Schedule a quarterly meeting with your investment adviser to review your investment goals and to evaluate your portfolio's performance. Each portion of your portfolio may need some tweaking and some changes to maintain a diversified, balanced portfolio that fits your needs perfectly.

Focus: Be vigilant about monitoring and maintaining your portfolio.

Day Three
Writing a Will

In movies the reading of the will is often the dramatic beginning to a murder mystery or a major family feud. Often the disposition of assets by a will is the motive for a murder. Why all this fuss over a written document? A will is the last written instruction left behind when you die. It legally tells the world, as well as your family and friends, what you want to give to whom.

Death brings with it a great deal of emotion: loss, abandonment, greed, love, fear, failure, desire, envy, jealousy, and more. Whether or not you want to accept it, no matter how much money you have or how many things you own, there will always be someone who thinks it belongs to them when you die.

"Great Aunt Susie left that painting to me. Uncle Tom gave me that shotgun before he died.

Aunt Susie gave me her engagement ring on her deathbed." It's amazing how people who think they should inherit an item can imagine that their beloved aunt, favorite uncle, or best friend, has the presence of mind to give away their valuables when they are barely conscious enough to recognize visitors while in their hospital bed. The only way to make sure that your money and your things go to the people you want to receive them is to make a personal gift while you are alive or specify it in writing as a part of your will.

Although you may feel you don't have much in the way of assets, writing a will is a good idea. What if your parents died and left you their home, cars, and savings? The minute you inherit those items you need a will to ensure that if you die, those things are passed on to the people or organizations you most want to inherit those things. As your life changes, whether you remain single, choose to marry, or have children, planning for an orderly distribution of your assets makes good sense.

When you write your will, you will name an executor (male) or executrix (female), who will be in charge of all your things after you die. If you have a house, a car, pets, children, your executrix or executor will make all the decisions about how to care for, manage, and feed those people and things left behind. Usually husbands and wives name their spouse as their executor, so that those decisions are handled in a way that is best for the remaining family members. Usually if there are children under eighteen years of age, a guardian is named in the will to address an event where both parents die simultaneously. If you are single, you may name a parent, sibling, or best friend to serve as your executor. You want someone you can trust to carry out your wishes as you've stated them in your will. Naming someone guardian over your children or the executor of your estate is a big responsibility, so make sure you ask before you do so, and make sure they understand what you expect of them.

If you don't have a will, the state you live in has a plan for those assets and a long, tedious and expensive process for distributing them to your potential heirs, or to the state itself. You can write a will in your own handwriting, called a holographic will, but there are specific rules about witnesses that have to be adhered to for a holographic will to be valid.

A simple will can be drawn up by most any licensed attorney in the state where you live. Estate planning attorneys can help with more complicated assets and utilize trusts and other techniques to protect assets where minor children are involved or family businesses need to be held together.

Once your will is written, make sure that you understand what it says and that it says what you want done for those you leave behind. Although you can change your will anytime you want, it is a good idea to share with your executor or executrix what your plans are as they are laid out in your will.

Writing a will, appointing someone whom you trust to be in charge, is one of the most loving things you can do for your family and friends. It takes the uncertainty out of their future, and leaves behind good memories of you for them.

Focus: Part of taking care of yourself financially is planning ahead for your inevitable death. The most loving thing you can do for your family and friends who are left behind after you are gone is to write a will.

Day Four

Healthcare Decisions in the Event of an Accident

Directive to Physician, Durable Power of Attorney for Healthcare, and Powers of Attorney

What happens to you if you are in a car accident? What if you can't communicate what you want the medical staff to do for you? How far do you want the medical staff to go to save your life? Most emergency staff members will do all they can to keep you alive, but there are points in treatment when tough decisions have to be made about your life, and you may not be alert enough to communicate what you want to those who are caring for you.

Writing and signing a Directive to Physician is the procedure to go through for you to specify what measures you want them to employ. Working hand in hand with this document is the Durable Power of Attorney for Healthcare, where you name one to two individuals to be in charge of your healthcare decisions in the event you are unable to make those decisions. Do you want a respirator? Do you want a feeding tube? Do you want a machine to breathe for you? Do you want to be resuscitated? How long do you want to be kept alive if you are in a coma?

Before signing the Directive to Physician and the Durable Power of Attorney for Healthcare, make sure the documents say what you want them to say, and make sure you understand what will happen if they are in force when there is an emergency. Understand what you are signing before you sign the documents.

By specifying in the Directive what you want and discussing it with the individuals you name in the Durable Power, you take a lot of pressure off of your family and loved ones, because they know what you want and how far you want to go. There is less drama and tension because it is clear what you want. Giving your chosen appointees the power to make healthcare decisions for you with the guidance of the Directive to Physician is one of the best ways you can care for yourself and your family.

Just as the Durable Power of Attorney for Healthcare comes in force when you are unable to make your own healthcare decisions, there is another document that also helps out when you are too ill or mentally disabled to manage your own assets: the Durable Power of Attorney. Usually for a Durable Power of Attorney to be enforceable, it requires that a number of doctors determine that you are not competent to manage your financial and personal affairs. You might be in a coma, have meningitis or suffer a stroke or dementia, and lose the ability to manage your everyday activities, such as paying bills, running your household, making business decisions, or other activities essential for continuing healthy daily living. If you do not have a Power of Attorney, then if you need a guardian, the court in your area will appoint someone to take care of your affairs----maybe someone you don't know, or maybe someone you know but don't want handling your financial and personal life.

In drafting this document, you name one or more individuals to manage your affairs until you are able to return to taking care of yourself. Keep in mind that if you do not recover, this individual may be in charge of your affairs forever, so in selecting a person make sure you trust them to have your best interests at heart. A parent, sibling, spouse, or best friend may be the right person for you, providing they have some business acumen and seem to be managing their own money and assets fairly well. If you do not know of anyone you trust in that regard, consider your accountant, banker, or investment advisor or a local trust company. Before you name this person or corporate entity, please discuss with them their willingness to do this for you in the event you need their help. Discuss your own strategies and how you keep your financial records, and where to find that information in the event you are unable to tell them where to look.

Executing a Durable Power of Attorney helps you take care of yourself when you are least able to do so, and when you need it the most. A well-ordered transition for the management of your assets will make things easier for you when you regain your health, or for your heirs in the event of your death.

Focus: Executing a Directive to Physician and a Durable Power of Attorney for Healthcare addresses your healthcare decisions when you can't make them. A Durable Power of Attorney for business affairs addresses your financial and personal life. These are responsible ways to take care of yourself and your family in the event you are incompetent to make those decisions yourself.

Day Five
Identity Theft

Every day someone is trying to find out your personal information, like your date of birth, Social Security number, bank account numbers, credit card numbers, passport numbers, driver's license number, and more. You must do all you can to protect that vital information from someone stealing your identity by using your information as if it was their own.

Whenever you are asked for your Social Security number by someone other than a prospective employer, financial institution, educational institution, or governmental agency, ask why they need that information and what safeguards they have in place to protect your information. If they don't have a reason that involves a background check, government requirement, or tie-in with your health insurance policy, then tell them to skip to the next question, or leave it blank on the form.

Beware of scams on the Internet or by phone that call stating there are problems with your bank or credit card accounts that require you to provide your account number, Social Security numbers or any other private information. If you receive such a notice, then call your bank or credit card company, using the number you find on your statement or on the back of the card, to find out if there is a real problem or someone is just "phishing." One reason to have a limited number of accounts and credit cards is so that there is no confusion about which card or which account may be affected.

Remember to keep your credit cards, debit cards, and identity cards, like your driver's license or passport, in a safe place. Keep them with you in your purse or wallet, or in a safe, a safety deposit box, or some other secure location. Make photocopies of the front and back of your cards, ID, and passport so you can notify the issuer and authorities to cancel them if they are stolen. Keep track of your cards like you keep track of your money.

If you use checks, make sure you keep them locked up when not in use. Use them in the numerical order in which you receive them, so if one is stolen from the middle of the pack you can easily tell from your bank statement that the check was used out of order. If you find you are missing checks, notify your bank immediately to put a hold on your account until you can establish a new account.

Many credit/debit card fraud occurrences take place at restaurants and bars where patrons give the server their card to take care of their tab. During the time your card is absent from your wallet, it can be copied, and later a clever thief can use it. Keep your receipts and compare them with the charges on your statement. Report any charges that you suspect were not made by you. Most likely you will not have to pay for those transactions and your financial institution will issue you a new card. If you are going out for a night of partying, it may be better to pay with cash rather than risk losing your card or your data to a potential thief.

Keeping your bank and credit card statements in a secured location is best for protecting your financial identity. Not only do those documents show the amount of money you have, but they also contain your address, Social Security number, and account number. For tax purposes you should keep copies of these documents for seven years, in the event you need to respond to an audit by the Internal Revenue Service. When you clean your files each year, make sure to shred these old statements with a cross-cut shredder, making it almost impossible to recover any of the physical information.

If you dispose of any computers with personal or financial information on the hard drive, pay to have the drive erased by a professional who can wipe the drive clean for a small fee before you dispose of them. Horror stories abound of individuals who donated computers to charity, only to find out that personal information remained on the hard drive, accessible to anyone who used the donated machine.

Focus: Guard your personal information that is essential to your financial identity. Remember to secure your ID cards, passport, credit cards, checks, and bank and credit account statements, as well as your computer.

Day Six

You, Your Phone, and the Internet

The Internet is both a blessing and a curse. You can look up anything you want for a research paper, a recipe, a shopping trip, a vacation, entertainment, and more. You can also look up information about yourself and other people. If you are just starting out in life, there may not be a lot out there about you, but maybe that is a good thing. Once you put it on the Internet, it is out there and you can't make it go away. Yes, someone may have to work very hard to find it, but with computer algorithms, that gets easier and faster everyday.

Posting on social media the latest pictures of your spring break trip has consequences. Prospective employers, college admissions departments, and others now have access to your most private moments when you choose to share them. Be discreet about what you post on social media—think about what others will think about what you say, how you look, and the "spin" you are putting on your life through that electronic billboard. It never goes away; once you post it, it is out in the public arena forever.

When you watch shows that "spin" politicians' and celebrities' lives, keep in mind that by their own choosing they are making their lives a public place, open to all kinds of scrutiny, unprotected by laws against defamation of character, slander, and libel. They have already given up their control over their images and control over their privacy. You still have a choice about what you do and how you portray yourself. Sharing too much may haunt you for a lifetime. Slutty pictures of girls smoking cigarettes and holding alcoholic beverages in photographs at parties, obvious drunken behavior captured on film, not to mention bragging about any of the above in postings on your social media pages, have very high costs for your future. You could be locked out of the future of your dreams by attempting to look like a big shot or celebrity when you are not one.

Using your phone to share sexy pictures of yourself with others, known as sexting, can come back to you in a negative way. Bullying through text messages, phone calls, and Internet postings is a behavior that alienates you from other people and can harm others. Treat other people the way you would like to be treated, with respect and dignity, when using electronic media and gadgets.

Do not use the Internet for pleasure or business if you are under the influence of alcohol or medications. Mistakes you make in an email, bad judgment during a shopping spree, and indiscreet revelations on your social media page can damage your reputation and create havoc in your personal and financial life.

Limit your time on the Internet for business and pleasure. Stop your usage of search engines, email, and social media at least an hour before you go to sleep to give your brain and body a chance to relax. Do not use your mobile phone when you are dining with other people or out for an evening with friends. If you must take a phone call, excuse yourself from the table and go outside or to a lobby area to complete your call. Don't expect everyone else to stop what they are doing so you can do business or be social on their time. Pay attention to the real people who are with you. Make conversation. Ask questions about what interests the others with you have outside of work and school.

Learn from each other. Be in the moment at the moment.

Focus: Think about your actions and decisions and the consequences of those choices. Limit your use of mobile phones in public. Be thoughtful about social media postings, text messages, emails, and phone calls. Remember: your life timeline is a long one, and you build your life one decision at a time.

Day Seven
Document, Document, Document

Throughout your life you will have a variety of experiences, some good and some bad. From time to time, you may find it helps to give compliments, make complaints, and keep notes about situations that are not working out the way you would like them to.

Keep files or notebooks on appliances, cars, or equipment you buy. File any receipts and warranty information in that location. When you need to have repairs done, then file the bills/receipts along with that information to refer to in the future. Notes about any problems not repaired should go along with these files. Any notes about service dates, conversations regarding service, and customer representative comments are part of the records you should keep.

When you find you are dissatisfied with a situation----maybe you had repair work done on an appliance, and three weeks later it is having the same problem, coinciding with the arrival of the bill for the original work----then you have to be your own advocate. Start with the customer service department, explain your situation, and give them a chance to fix it. If the warranty period for the work done is over, then you may need to evaluate whether fixing it again is a good idea; maybe buying a new product is a better choice. If not, then ask for the repair to be done a second time, as soon as possible. As you interact with customer relations, make a note of the date, the time, and the name of the person with whom you spoke and what was promised or stated in the conversation. Staple that information to the bill and put it in your notebook or file.

If you receive exemplary service, take the time to write a note to the owner of the company or the immediate supervisor of the service representative about the great service provided by their employee. Make a note of the individual who helped you and ask for them in the future if they are still in that position. Thank the individual who helped you and remember their name. Many corporations keep track of customers who take the time to give compliments for good service. Often it can result in an upgrade in service or more prompt attention in the future. Besides, everyone likes to get compliments.

Most work environments have procedures for dealing with problems in the workplace. Whether it is sexual harassment, discrimination, or personal differences, there is usually a process to go through for addressing a problem you may have with your supervisor, your work environment, or your compensation. Remember to keep your cool and stay calm whenever you are confronted with a difficult work situation or bad evaluation. If you lose your temper, you will most likely be fired for cause. No one will defend bad behavior.

If you are suffering at work, then follow the procedure specified. Keep a diary with dates, names, times, and details of the problematic events that occurred. Copies of ugly emails, recordings of hateful messages, and notes about events that were inappropriate are important documentation you will need to make your case about your problem. Remember to maintain your composure in all your dealings with any bad actors. It may be hard to do, but it will be to your benefit later on when you are looking for help.

These same techniques work if you have a car that is turning out to be a lemon: you will need to document the work history and the problems that just can't seem to be fixed. Keeping a good paper trail that answers the questions of who, what, when, where, and why is the best defense and offense you can have if you have to fight for your rights.

Focus: Document, document, document. Keep a record of time, date, place, person, and conversation when you are dealing with persistent problems that affect your personal and professional life.

Legal Matters

1. Read and understand everything you sign. Remember to "read the rulebook."

2. Write a will.

3. Execute a Directive to Physician, Durable Power of Attorney for Healthcare, and a Durable Power of Attorney for your business affairs.

4. Review and verify the information regularly on your monthly bank and credit statements.

5. Safeguard your personal financial information.

6. Protect your image on the Internet.

7. Refrain from using cell phones when you are socializing with others.

8. Document, document, document.

Week Seven: Renting an Apartment or House

The first time you move away from home you will be renting a place to live. It may be an apartment or house you share with others, or a little room of your own. Whatever you first nest is, let it be your base camp for your journey out into the world. Make it a place where you can find comfortable surroundings, nourishing food, and a playground for your soul. Your home should be a place that sustains you, refreshes you, and prepares you for your climb up the mountain of life.

Day One

Selecting a Place to Live

Location, location, and location: the first rule in real estate is that location matters. When you are looking for an apartment or house to rent, usually the location is the most important factor in deciding whether to rent it. Is it close to work or school? Is it on a bus line or close to the subway stop? Can you walk to work or school? Are there grocery stores, pharmacies, restaurants, and cleaners nearby?

Once you've figured out the area you are interested in, then the question of whether you can afford it comes into play. Spending more than twenty-five percent of your take-home pay on your rent may put you at risk for being cash poor at the end of the month. It may limit what you can spend on other things, like entertainment or eating out, so you may wish to be careful not to spend too much when looking for an apartment.

Safety is another factor to evaluate. Are there bars on the windows? Is it located in an area with a high crime rate? When you look up police reports for that area, are there a great number of violent crimes against people or crimes against property? Are there designated parking places, or do you have to park on the street? How far away is your parking spot from the front door of your residence? Is there lighting that comes on at dusk and stays on until dawn? Do you know anyone else who lives in the complex? How close are you to the street? How close are you to the manager's office? The mailboxes? The vending machines? If it is an apartment complex, is it gated, with controlled access? Take a tour of the complex, the parking lots, and any other common area. How is it maintained? How does it feel to you? Do you feel safe in the area where the apartment is located? Will you have any privacy?

If you have more than one roommate or if you have a pet, you may decide to rent a house or townhouse that has a yard or area where you can sit outside and your pet can play. Like an apartment, select a house for the same reasons: location, safety, and nearby amenities. Unlike an apartment, a house may come with more maintenance responsibilities. There may not be a maintenance person on site, so you may be the one who has to arrange for the plumber to come, or for air-conditioning repair.

Also, there may be a yard to mow or a pool to clean, which you can delegate to a service or do yourself, depending on the time and money you have available and the agreement with the homeowner.

Focus: Select an apartment or house that you would be happy living in for quite a while. Make sure it is in a location that pleases you for work, school, or play.

Day Two
Roommates

Once you find the area you want to be in, determine the safety of the neighborhood, and figure out what you can afford to spend on an apartment, then you may want to consider whether you need a roommate or can live alone. Having a roommate may allow you to live in a nicer apartment or complex, save some money, and have company when you don't have other plans. However, if you do have a roommate, set up some ground rules about how you are going to share responsibilities from the beginning.

Besides the issues of who gets the larger bedroom or the en suite bath, discuss in advance how the rent, utility, and Internet expenses will be divided between you. Do you plan to share groceries and the refrigerator communally, or will you each have separate food and shelves? Will you each furnish your own rooms? Will you share the cost of a sofa, TV, dining table and chairs? Who will take out the trash and recycling? Who will clean the kitchen? Vacuum the carpet? Do your best to work on these issues beforehand; otherwise, later on you may find yourself in the middle of a lot of ugly arguments.

Focus: If you have a roommate, discuss responsibilities in advance. Try using a job jar if you can't agree, randomly selecting your chores each week from a jar filled with slips of paper each one naming a different job around the apartment.

Day Three

The Lease

Once you've identified the apartments or houses that interest you, ask for a copy of the lease you will be required to sign. Read the lease carefully. Pay special attention to the term of the lease; is it six months, twelve months, or longer? Is the rent rate a fixed rate for the term of the lease? When is the rent due? When is the rent considered late? Are utilities included in the rent you pay? What about water? Is there an extra charge, known as a surcharge, that is passed on to you if it is included in the rent? When the lease is about to expire, usually the tenant must give notice of the intent to renew or to move out. The lease will tell you if it is a month, two months, a week or two weeks before the lease runs out. Often there is a provision for month-to-month renting after the lease expires, but that may involve an automatic rent increase with an escalation clause that allows the rent to increase each month thereafter automatically.

Look for sections of the lease that deal with repairs and maintenance. As the tenant, are you responsible for new light bulbs, air filters, and paying for plumbing and appliance repairs as well? If you are renting a house, is the landlord taking care of the yard and pool maintenance, or is that your responsibility? If it is not addressed in the lease, make sure you create some written agreement that you and the landlord both sign in order to clarify who is responsible for what maintenance. Take into account extra expenses when figuring your monthly outlay for housing based on those additional financial responsibilities.

In addition, there may be special sections of the lease that addresses rules regarding flame-burning candles or live Christmas trees in the unit. In areas prone to flooding or excessive amounts of rain, tenants are required to notify management immediately if there is water damage or evidence of mold on walls or carpeting. Pay attention to this kind of language, since it gives you a clue that it's better to live in an upper-floor unit as opposed to a ground-floor unit in an area prone to water rising in heavy downpours. Use the lease as a tool to make a good decision about where you plan to live.

A lease usually requires a deposit of the rent amount for the first month and the last month. Sometimes there are additional deposits for pets, parking places, or other additional amenities associated with the apartment. Verify whether these deposits are refundable at the end of your lease. Learn under what conditions they will not be refunded. Even though you may have paid the last month's rent as a deposit at the beginning, you are expected to pay the rent when it is normally due the last month of your lease. The last month's rent deposit is held until the apartment is inspected after you have moved out and, if necessary will be used to repair any damage to the unit that was sustained while you lived there.

Focus: Read and understand the lease before you sign it. If any part of it is unclear to you, ask questions and get clarification of what the language in the lease means.

Day Four
The Pre-lease Walk-Through

Before you sign the lease and before you move in, walk through the apartment or house that you will be renting. Take note of any existing damage to carpeting, walls, appliances, and fixtures. Document the damage with a photograph to provide proof that the problem existed before you moved in. Make sure that all the appliances work: does the stovetop heat up, is the refrigerator cold, is the freezer working, do the faucets work, can you get hot water from the tap? Check to see if there are smoke alarms by the bedrooms and confirm who maintains them. Are the toilets, baths, and sinks clean or are they stained and rusted?

Focus: To protect yourself when you move out, document the condition of the rental property before you move in.

Day Five

Deposits and Insurance

Most landlords require a deposit of at least one month's rent in order to secure an apartment for future rental. Once you sign a lease, you may be required to give an additional month's deposit, usually referred to as the last month's rent, which the landlord may hold to cover damages to your apartment once you've moved out. If the utilities are not included in the rent, there may be additional deposits required to set up electric and gas utilities, water, Internet, cable or satellite television, and telephone. All of these deposits can be refunded to you if you move out of the service area for those providers. Keep a log of your deposits so you can follow up later to collect that money after you move.

Pet deposits are usually one-time permanent, non-refundable deposits that are used to repair any damage your pets do to drapes, woodwork, carpet, or walls. In addition, a landlord may use this money to fumigate your apartment after you've left to rid it of any pests like fleas and ticks. You may be required to provide evidence that your pet has all its vaccinations and that it is currently on flea or tick prevention when you make the application for your pet to reside with you in your apartment or house rental.

Do not "hide" a pet from the landlord, since as a tenant your unit can be entered at any time for maintenance. It would be an ugly surprise to have your dog Rover, unknown to management, accost the air-conditioning repairman when he comes into your unit to replace the air filter. It may also result in your eviction from the place where you live, forfeiting your rental deposit along with the pet deposit. Fill out the pet deposit application and pay the required fee. If you have a dog, keep it secured in a kennel in your apartment while you are away to protect it from surprise guests. Cats will usually hide under the bed, but take precautions if you think it might run out the door.

Whenever you are renting an apartment or a house, consider tenant's insurance to protect your furniture, clothing, and personal property from fire, theft, or other damage. If there is a plumbing leak that drenches your clothes in a closet and they all have to be replaced, you will have insurance to cover it. The landlord takes no responsibility for your personal items and the replacement of them in the event of a catastrophe. Although this is an additional expense to include in your budget, it may be worth it for peace of mind alone.

Focus: Deposits and insurance are additional expenses to consider when you rent. Keep track of your deposits in order to have them refunded to you when you move out or when you move to a different geographic area.

Day Six

What Your Landlord Expects of You

Just because you don't own the place does not mean you can destroy it without consequences. The better care you take of the apartment or house you rent, the more likely you will be to get your deposit back when you move out. If you are in an apartment complex, your neighbors will appreciate your keeping your place clean and bug free. Take out the trash on a regular basis and remove science experiments from the refrigerator. When the food starts to grow green fuzz on it, that is definitely a sign it is past its prime. Keep the kitchen counters wiped down and the sink clean. Minimize the temptation to roaches and ants to come live in your apartment with you.

Regular cleaning of the toilet, bathtubs, and sinks will make it easier to prepare your apartment for the landlord's inspection at your departure. You will also cut down on the number of colds and vanquish stomach bugs that might attack your immune system.

If there are plumbing leaks or problems with appliances, report them to the maintenance department and management immediately. If your air conditioner is working overtime, or if you smell gas when your heater is operating, make sure these are checked for problems. Make every effort to be cooperative with the landlord.

Be a good neighbor and watch the volume on your music and your guests. Loud parties will cause someone to call the police and complain, drawing attention to you and damaging your reputation.

Even if an appliance isn't working, there is no excuse for destroying it. Just ask the manager to fix it. Be careful moving in and out to avoid damage to walls, floors, carpets, and ceilings. If you have a pet that has accidents, use a cleaning solution that removes urine, vomit, and fecal matter as soon as the problem comes to your attention. Consider limiting your pet's access to only tile floors in your unit or house.

Being considerate of your neighbors and your landlord will create better living conditions for you. At year-end, near the holidays, you may want to make cookies for the manager or the maintenance staff to let them know how much you appreciate them and what they do for you.

Focus: Be a responsible tenant by taking care of your living space, keeping it clean and operational.

Day Seven
Moving Out

Once you know that you will be moving on to another location, give notice to your landlord in the manner that is specified in the lease and in the time required in the lease agreement. Plan your move to give yourself three days to a week to clean up the unit. Give yourself time to clean out the refrigerator and wipe it down with disinfectant, clean all the toilets, tubs, and sinks, and vacuum and mop the floors. Remember to replace any curtains or other moveable items that you may have removed during your tenancy.

Start by packing your clothes and personal items, separating the items that you may not want anymore and plan to give away or sell. Wash any dirty clothes, sheets, and towels, leaving only what you will need for the last days you will live in the unit. If you are not taking all your furniture, then give away or sell the items you will not be keeping. Do not leave clothes, personal items, or furniture in your unit for the landlord to deal with once you have left.

Once you have moved all boxes, clothes, and furniture from the unit, make one last check to be sure all closets, laundry rooms, bathrooms, and cupboards are empty and clean.

Take pictures of your unit to have for your records in the event you have a problem with the return of your deposits.

Usually landlords hold on to the deposit for a month before returning it. Your lease may specify how you can request the return of your deposit. Making a request in writing or online directing them to send your deposit to your new address will simplify things for you and the landlord. Keep a copy of your email or letter for your files, in the event there is a dispute over the return of the deposit.

Focus: Leave the apartment or house you rented in at least the same condition as you found it when you first moved in, if not better.

Renting an Apartment or House

1. Select a place that is a good location for your needs.

2. If you have a roommate, discuss your financial, housekeeping, and social responsibilities with each other before you live together

3. Read the lease before you sign it. Look for clues that may help you choose between one location and another. Know what you can and cannot do in your apartment.

4. Before you move in, document the condition of the rental with photographs and notations.

5. If you have a pet, pay the deposit and submit the application before you move in.

6. Purchase tenant's insurance for your personal possessions.

7. Keep you rental clean and free of trash.

8. Be considerate of your neighbors, the maintenance staff, and the property management.

9. Notify management as soon as possible of any problems in your unit: broken appliances, gas leaks, water leaks, heating and air-conditioning malfunctions, and so on.

10. Allow a week to move out of your rental. Organize your move to ensure that you remove all personal possessions and leave the rental clean and free of trash.

11. Leave the rental in the same condition it was in when you moved in, or better.

Week Eight: Money before Marriage

At some time in your life you will fall in love or in lust with someone. The symptoms vary with every individual. You may not be able to sleep at night because all you can do is think about him or her. You might want to see that person all the time, you might lose your appetite, you might want to be close to them all the time or only see them from afar. Whatever your particular brand of lovesickness, do your best to step back and be rational before you make it a permanent relationship. The next three weeks explore topics you may want to discuss with the object of your affection before you move in together, tie the knot, or say vows promising to love and cherish each other forever and ever.

Day One

Falling In and Out of Love

One of the most expensive things you can do in life is get divorced. Not only is it expensive because the lawyers get most of the money in fees, but it is emotionally devastating and can have a lasting effect on your self-esteem and confidence, affecting your ability to trust another person, whether in a personal relationship or a business relationship. A divorce can also affect your earning potential for quite a while. So before you buy the ring, sign the papers, or make any commitment, talk about a whole lot of hypothetical situations to find out more about your partner than you knew before.

Relationships can break up for a lot of reasons----money troubles, infidelity, family disagreements, health problems, lack of love, boredom, and the catchall excuse of "irreconcilable differences" which covers a multitude of sins. Making any relationship last for a long time requires a great deal of work. Work on yourself in developing patience, kindness, understanding, and a willingness to extend yourself for another person. Besides developing a better personality, there is the work of being able to see yourself for who you really are. Recognize you are not an angel and work to figure out what you need to do to be a better person, whatever that is. Sometimes forgiveness of yourself and those who may have hurt you in the past can be a big part of the work of love. Letting go of the past, of always getting your way, of being right all the time, and of winning at the expense of others: all these actions are part of the work of love and essential to creating a loving relationship that can last. You don't have to be a doormat or stay in an abusive relationship. Find someone who has your best interests at heart and who is willing to work on your relationship with you. If you both work together, you have a chance for a lifelong relationship where you can build and grow a future together.

If you decide you want to move in together before you tie the knot, then draw up an agreement between the two of you regarding your cohabiting together. Specify who is responsible for what expenses and what chores. Make sure you are clear about how much you will each contribute to your joint living expenses. List what you each are bringing into the place you are going to live. Just in case it does not work out, you will clearly know what belongs to whom and how much one of you may owe the other. Use your head and come up with an agreement you can live with.

Focus: Don't let love and lust lead you into a relationship that will bring you pain in a few years. Take time to get to know your beloved before you are in a permanent relationship.

Day Two

How Do You Each Spend Money?

When you first meet someone who is attractive to you, there are qualities that you can still remember weeks after your first meeting. The color of their eyes, their smile, maybe their great physique is what you noticed first. During those first few times that you get together, for coffee, or a movie, maybe dinner or a glass of wine, did you notice how money was spent? Are you both paying your own way? Are you taking turns treating one another to a movie or dinner? Is one of you throwing money around like it is water? Are you both being careful with how much you are spending? Who is paying cash? Are credit cards the preferred means of paying for an evening out? Does it feel like one of you is trying a little too hard to impress? Or is one of you acting as if you are entitled to the good things in life? Are your get-togethers at country clubs or other private clubs? Or are you both scouring the current events in your town to find a free movie, lecture, or dance? Do you use coupons? Does your beloved consider retailing a sport? Does he or she buy on sale, or buy whatever they want whenever they want?

Take the time to observe how your object of affection spends money. Open up the conversation about financial goals, personal ambitions, the perfect life to lead. Find out how your ideas of saving and spending mesh. Talk about life goals and expectations.

Play the "what if" game. What if you won the lottery? What would you do with the money? Would you spend all the money on yourselves? Would you give it away to charity? Would you save some? Spend it on others? Buy your dream house? Travel? This is a good way to learn about each other and your respective attitudes about money.

Often, when a person goes from rags to riches, their moral compass will change and they will believe that because they are rich they are above the law and are not subject to the rules everyone else abides by. Some people think that because they have a lot of money they are more intelligent than people who do not have as much money as they have. If you are wealthy or hobnobbing with the well to do, beware of your attitude toward respecting others and rules in general. Financial success can sometimes open the door for infidelity, attitudes of entitlement, and inconsideration of others.

Focus: Pay attention to the basic attitudes about money that are expressed by your beloved. How does it mesh with your own?

Day Three
How Much Do I Owe?

A majority of students in college take on student loan debt, racking up as much as $100,000 in debt or more before they graduate. Before student loans were such big business for banks and educational institutions, students worked their way through college with part-time jobs, often extending the years to get their degree to eight to ten years. Now the issue is whether students can earn enough money to pay off the loans in a timely fashion.

When two students with student loan debt fall in love, they double up on the debt they are responsible for, affecting their future ability to borrow money to purchase a residence, save for college for their own children, and save for their own retirement. Knowing how much student loan debt your beloved is responsible for and what their plan is to pay that debt back is important. If you have student loan debt, what is your plan for paying it off? Have you decided how much you want to pay off each year for the next ten years? Are you looking at taking a second job in order to pay the debt off faster? Are you willing to give up your daily latte or weekly movie in order to pay it off faster? Break up the total into smaller more manageable amounts and celebrate each time you reach a milestone and diminish the debt. After the debt is paid off, think about the extra money you'll have to spend on something you want or to save for something special.

Focus: Identify and share your debt situation with the one you love. Have a plan for paying off the debt. If you don't each have a plan, then develop one together. Help and encourage one another in becoming free of debt.

Day Four
Taxes

In life, the only two things you have to do are pay taxes and die. The Treasury Department, also known as the Internal Revenue Service, collects taxes all of the time. Once you accept that taxes will be withheld from your income or that you will be required to pay estimated income taxes, your life will be much simpler. Don't fight it, just do it.

Unfortunately, a lot of people like to keep all of their earned income and don't pay taxes, so they find themselves in trouble with the IRS. This can lead to forced withholding from any banking and investment accounts, as well as the freezing and the ultimate sale of other assets, including real estate, art, and securities.

Make sure you are up-to-date with the IRS, and check to make sure your beloved is too, before you enter into any legal partnership. Someone who has not filed tax returns, or who has not paid the taxes due for years, may have a large balance, with penalties and interest due payable to the Treasury Department. Maybe ignorance is the excuse, or a difficult time in life, but once you are formally linked together, you will be responsible for the money due, possibly creating resentments and problems later in your relationship.

If you or your partner-to-be owns any real estate----a home, commercial property, or raw land----make sure the property taxes are up-to-date. Look up the real estate address or the name of the owner on the taxing authority website for that region, and the tax record will be evident. A balance due will be shown or a zero amount listed. Taxing authorities can force the sale of real property in order to meet the tax obligations due. Property taxes are usually paid once per year, with some taxing authorities permitting semi-annual, quarterly, or monthly payments. Many mortgage companies include the property taxes in the mortgage payment amount and then make that payment for the homeowner each year. If that is the case for you, then make sure the mortgage company takes care of that tax obligation by checking the taxing authority website for your property and following up with your mortgage company if there is a problem with payment.

Focus: Income taxes and property taxes must be paid; otherwise valuable assets and even your home may be sold out from under you.

Day Five

Consumer Debt

Credit cards and personal charge accounts may be convenient for you to use, but it is best to pay them off each month. If your true love uses credit cards frequently when shopping, dining, or traveling, find out if they are paying off the totals each month or just making the minimum payment. At interest rates ranging from five percent to twenty-five percent, the total balance due can quickly compound to double or triple the original amount charged on an account or card. Statements from credit companies can "hide" the total amount, prominently displaying the minimum amount due as if it is the total amount due. Check your statements, make sure all the charges are yours, and then pay the total amount due each month.

If you have a large amount of credit card debt, or if your partner does, then stop using the credit cards, placing them in a drawer, safe, or in a glass of water in the freezer, to stop you from impulse spending. Then take the total amount you owe and divide it into manageable monthly payments, paying off the amount a bit at a time, until the total amount is paid off.

Focus: Acknowledge your credit card and charge account debt. Make a plan to pay it off and do so as quickly as possible. Do not use your cards again until after the debt is fully paid.

Day Six
Other Financial Responsibilities

If you fall in love with an older, more experienced person, they may have additional monthly financial responsibilities that affect your lifestyle once your relationship is permanent. If they own a home, there may be a monthly mortgage to pay, along with real estate taxes and insurance to protect that investment. If a previous marriage or relationship is part of their history, there may be monthly alimony or child support payments. Both of you need to be honest about your financial obligations before you become permanent parts of each other's lives.

Are there other responsibilities that can exact a toll on your joint finances? Is there a child who will be living in your home part-time or full-time, needing food, clothing, books and toys, and health care, as well as childcare? Maybe your partner has a beloved pet along with that pet's vet bills, food costs, grooming expenses, and playtime needs. Is there an elderly parent or grandparent whose care will be your responsibility? Find out what your household income and expenses will look like once you come together as a couple.

Focus: Familial obligations have a financial side to them. Explore the possibilities and know what to expect once you are together.

Day Seven
Funds for Frills

Planning for the delightful, the frivolous, and the fun is an important part of nurturing a happy relationship. When you are discussing your dreams and hopes for your new union, take time to share your ideas about your fantasy of the perfect night out or perfect date night. What will you spend on that gala evening or that quiet dinner and concert? Save for it. Create a line item in your expense plan or budget for your weekly night out. If you know your ideal date requires one hundred dollars a week, then put aside twenty dollars a day. If that is living a bit too rich, then set aside less, but plan for one really special night once a month. Four dollars a day saved, the price of a fancy coffee drink, will buy you a nice evening out once a month.

There will be a time when one of you really wants something new, like a new dress, new tool, new fishing rod, new furniture, new car, or new boat. Before you make the plunge to humor your inner child that wants, wants, wants, talk about it with your best pal. If you get to spend one thousand dollars that is not included in the spending plan, then does your partner get to do the same? How are you going to handle these situations? Is one of you always going to get what he or she wants while the other builds up resentment and feels like they are the lesser partner in the relationship? Discuss and figure out how the two of you together are going to deal with these big expenses or bigger circumstances before they happen and throw your financial plans and your relationship into a crisis. Plan and save for those special wants, making it a treat, not a terror.

Everyone needs to get away from day-to-day life on occasion----to leave work behind for a few days or let the kids stay with a sitter, to take a vacation. A vacation can be as simple as staying in town, turning off the phones, computers, email and Internet, and exploring your own community, taking time for naps, spa services, special events, and dinners out. Some people love the beach at a wonderful resort by turquoise seas; others like the mountains and skiing down the sparkling, snowy slopes. Whatever your idea of a blissful vacation may be, then set up a vacation fund and save for it. Break it down into small amounts and figure out what you need to put aside each day, each week, each month, in order to take a little time off when you and your beloved need to get away from reality and put the magic back into your relationship.

Focus: Plan for the special treats, dates, and trips in your lives together. Remember you can have an expense plan or budget with fun built into your plan. Make fun intentional in your lives together, not just a leftover accident.

Money before Marriage

1. Marriage takes work.
2. Take time to get to know your beloved.
3. Learn how to talk about money together.
4. How do you each spend money? Carelessly or carefully?
5. Find out how much student loan debt you each have.
6. Does either of you owe taxes to the IRS? If so, make a plan to pay that debt off.
7. If you have real property, does either of you owe taxes on it? If so, plan to pay it.
8. How many credit cards do you each have? How much credit card debt do you each have? Pay it off before you tie the knot.
9. Discuss any family responsibilities you have or will have. Do you have child support or alimony payments due? How will you pay for those expenses?
10. Do either of you have any savings? Any retirement plans?

11. What do you have budgeted to spend on a monthly basis? How will that change once you marry?

12. Do either of you plan to work for an advanced degree? How will you pay for that expense?

13. Plan and save for special wants, dates together, and get-away vacations.

Week Nine: Before the Wedding

A good friend of mine, Sara, was in her thirties, married once before, and fell in love with a professional man, Aaron, a Jew. Sara was raised in the Christian faith but had Jewish friends, so she was comfortable with their religious differences. As their dating progressed, they discussed having children and the faith tradition in which they would be raised. Aaron declared that the faith of the mother determined the faith of the children. Once they were engaged, Sara attended the conversion class at the local reform synagogue with the intention of converting to Judaism.

The rabbi announced at the first meeting that if one was converting because of the possibility of marriage, then both members of the couple had to attend the classes. Aaron was busy working late much of the time, so he abdicated his responsibility to his future mate and did not attend the classes. Sara did quite well, learning about Judaism and the various sacraments and prayers, some of which she delightfully discovered were the foundation for the Christian sacraments she grew up with as a child. She converted to Judaism, they were married, and then the problems began.

Sara worked hard to put together the Friday Sabbath dinner, with the lighting of the candles and the blessing of the wine and bread. She observed a day of fasting on Yom Kippur, attended services on Rosh Hashanah and Yom Kippur. She even followed the prescribed Jewish mourning rituals when her father, a non-Jew, died. Ironically, the more Sara tried to create the perfect Jewish home life for her husband, the more absent he was. Finally, when she confronted him about his wanting a Jewish wife and a Jewish mother for his children, he explained that his family practiced the religion in the secular tradition but were not active in the spiritual faith or as a lifestyle. Sara was working to be a religious Jew, interjecting the Jewish faith in their everyday life.

Had Aaron attended the classes and had they both discussed their expectations about how, why, when, and with whom they would practice their religion before they married, things might have been better off from the beginning. They might have avoided the divorce they ultimately lived through.

Day One

Your Individual Spiritual Beliefs

Whether you do or don't have a spiritual life or spiritual beliefs can certainly affect the success of your union with another individual. Attending religious services as a regular part of your weekly life, making time for daily meditation, tithing to an organized church or synagogue, delving into the power of the universe through personal exploration: all these are examples of different aspects of spiritual life. Before you cement your relationship and are committed to it, explore each other's spiritual lives.

Make it a game of Twenty Questions. When you were a child did you go to services each week? Once a week or more often? Were you in the choir? Did you teach/take Sunday school classes? How much time do you currently spend with Bible study? Do you engage in a daily or weekly meditation? Do you say a grace before meals? Do you believe in the Holy Trinity? What kind of religious jewelry do you wear and why? Would you be willing to convert to another religion, or change branches of the Christian church? Have you done missionary work? If so, where? How do you feel about your missionary work? Are you an agnostic? Are you an atheist? If so, why? Please ask any other spiritually related questions to the one you love so you can better understand that part of their life before you live together.

Now that you know a bit more about the spiritual belief system of your future partner, consider whether you will affiliate yourselves with a specific spiritual or religious institution. Will this be a place where you will both attend services regularly? Will you be making a regular charitable contribution to this organization, possibly a tithe of ten percent of your income, or will you come to an agreement on another amount that might be more appropriate for your budget? Will your volunteer time, money, and energy be devoted solely to your spiritual institution, or will you be involved with other groups as well? How often will you attend services? Will you choose to be a member of the leadership of this group?

If you have agreed to be involved in different religious or spiritual institutions, how will you manage your time apart and your time together, your family obligations and work commitments, and how will you celebrate spiritual or religious holidays? Conversations about these topics will give you insight into how your lives together will unfold. Be respectful of each other's background and upbringing. Be open and detailed in describing your expectations and your hopes and dreams. Yes, these discussions may lead you to some disagreements or conflicts, but these need to be resolved before you legally bind yourselves to each other.

Focus: Find out the nature of the spiritual life of your future partner and share your beliefs as well. Share your past experience with religion and spirituality while growing up, and your expectations of how you imagine religion will play a part in your life together as a couple.

Day Two

How You Interact with Each Other

"He takes me for granted."

"She doesn't even kiss me goodbye anymore."

"He talks to me like I'm his servant."

"It's not only that we don't have sex. We don't even kiss or hug anymore."

Statements like these are uttered over a cup of coffee between girlfriends and over a beer by a couple of guys of all ages. It doesn't matter if you've been together for a year or forty years, how you interact with each other is a big part of keeping your love and your lust for each other alive.

When you stop saying "please" when you are asking for the rolls to be passed at the dinner table, or when you don't say "thank you," when your dinner plate steaming with food is placed before you, then you've started to take your partner for granted. When you interrupt each other, you aren't listening to each other. Everyone likes to be acknowledged and respected.

When your spouse comes home from work, or when you meet together to get dinner, do you hug and kiss and say, "I love you! I'm glad to see you!" Before you go to bed at night, do you share a goodnight kiss and wish each other "sweet dreams"? When you notice your mate has made a special effort to dress nicely, do their hair, put on makeup or aftershave, do you comment on how good they look and how nice it was for them to make the special effort with their appearance? We all need and want positive good vibes from the people we love.

Everyone is busy with work, school, volunteer activities, a social life, housekeeping, cooking, watching the kids, and driving from one place to another, so making time to tell each other that you still care, that you still think he is handsome or smart or a wonderful dad or that she still rocks your world, matters a lot.

If you feel like your schedule is making it hard to connect, then consider a little idea that allows you to decorate your loved one's life with your love. Multicolored sticky notes, inscribed with your positive thoughts, left on the bathroom mirror or by the door or on the TV remote or bedside table or on the fridge door, can give anyone a lift. When my husband would leave for a trip, I would hide notes in his suitcase for him to find. Sometimes it would be cards, other times just a sticky note, letting him know I was thinking of him and missed him while he was away.

If you are shying away from sex, maybe it is because it has become too ordinary, too rushed, or happens at the wrong time of day. If there is a two-year-old in the hall banging on the door to get into your bedroom, it will be hard for anyone to perform. Most women want to feel comforted, sexy, and valued. Some want to be romanced into sex with music, candlelight, and a loving touch. Many men want to feel they are stars in a porn movie, with their partner supplying all the appropriate dirty words and naughty outfits. Talk about what would make you both more interested in sexual activity with each other.

Find ways to show each other you care. Write a note, bring a flower, rub their shoulders, welcome each other home, and treat each other politely and lovingly. Compliment each other. If you don't know what to do, then ask for assistance from the object of your affection.

Focus: Find out what each of you needs for affection and attention. Give of yourself to the one you love.

Day Three
Health Issues

If you had a fatal disease, wouldn't it be nice to share that information with your future partner before your lives, money, and health are tied together? Are you a victim of a sexually transmitted disease, acquired during a sexual fling without proper protection from a source that didn't disclose their infection to you beforehand? Is there a history of mental illness in your family? Are you genetically predisposed to Down syndrome, cystic fibrosis, multiple sclerosis, bipolar disorder, ADHD, ADD, low sperm count, or sterility? Share your health histories with one another, even if there is something you are embarrassed about, because if there is a problem now, it will be a whole lot worse if you've covered it up or hidden it from the person you say you will love forever.

You may also want to share your family health histories as well. Is heart disease something you need to watch out for? Did your mother have breast cancer? Are your parents alcoholics? If there are major concerns on your part that may explain your diet, exercise program, or daily vitamin intake, then share those with the person you want to spend your life with.

If you and your partner are sexually active, what form of birth control do you use? Abstinence? Condoms? Rhythm method? Oral contraceptives? Vaginal ring? Intrauterine device? Vasectomy? Sub dermal implant? Have you discussed this together? Are you both familiar with how each method works and what side effects each one has? Planning a pregnancy to take place when you and your partner are ready, willing, and able to care for another human being by being loving, caring, financially responsible, and good parents is extremely important for stability in a relationship. If you are playing "baby roulette," taking a chance on pregnancy while being sloppy about contraception, you and your partner need to stop and think about what you are doing and why you are doing it. Let a baby come into your life when you can take care of it and love it----not as an accident, but as an intentional act of loving one another.

Are you both working to keep your bodies fit and strong? Is this something you do together or separately? How are you going to make sure exercise fits into your schedules when you add a family or have increased responsibilities at work? Discuss the possibility of getting up early to work out or taking a long walk after dinner or moving dinnertime to a later hour so each of you can take time out to stay fit.

By now you know if you are dating a meat-and-potatoes man or woman or a vegan with an affection for avocados. How do you plan meals around each other's food requirements and preferences? Who is going to cook and when? Who will clean up and when? How will you structure meal prep and mealtime to give each of you the diet that best suits your temperament, body, and attitudes about food?

Will alcohol be a part of your daily life? Cocktails before dinner and after work: will this be the norm? How about wine with dinner? Can one of you drink while the other abstains? What about recreational drugs? Do you both partake? Can one of you get high while the other chooses not to? Is smoking cigarettes okay with each of you? Cigars? A pipe? Can you smoke inside or only outside? Is one of you allergic? How will you work this out over time? Be open to discussion about these habits and additions to your life. Be honest with yourself and your partner about how you feel about his or her habits.

Focus: By disclosing your health history, your personal habits, and your attitudes about diet and exercise, you will be laying the groundwork for more openness in your relationship. Better to know your future spouse uses tobacco before you marry than afterward. Yes, these habits can change over time, but if you find you can accept your beloved as he or she is, chances are you will grow together over time.

Day Four
What about Family?

There is an old adage that when you marry a person, you also marry their family. You marry their prejudices and their grudges in addition to their sense of humor and their teasing. If his mom doesn't like you, or her father uses the F-bomb every other word, you will be marrying those people too. People can change, but it takes years, and there is no guarantee anyone will want to change for you. If you can't accept your partner's family, then think carefully about whether this is a good match for you.

Have you met each other's family members in their natural environment, in their homes? Before you visit for the first time, let your mate know what to expect when meeting your family of origin. Talk about what you like about your family and what you wish was different and why. If visiting for a weekend or longer, share with your sweetheart an idea of how much togetherness to expect, what kind of clothes to bring, what activities are planned.

When you first meet, pay attention to both positive and negative interactions. Good and bad habits may reveal themselves in the process. These qualities may subvert or enhance the family culture you and your beloved want to create. We all bring baggage into our relationships, and being aware of it can help address any stress that may arise due to conflicts in your respective upbringings.

How does your beloved interact with his or her parents? With his or her siblings? Does he or she become more childlike and less independent when they are with their family? Are there more conflicts due to sibling rivalry or parental prejudice? Are your needs and wishes disregarded by your beloved if they conflict with that of her or his family of origin? Can you tolerate this behavior when you are with them? Is there a hangover effect that lingers on after you two have returned to your normal life together? How can you handle this situation so that it allows you to resume your lives and grow together in the process, rather than apart?

How his or her parents and siblings treat and interact with you is very important. Do they show you respect? Do they listen and pay attention to what you are saying, or do they interrupt or change focus when you are speaking? Will you be dealt with as an outlaw or as an in-law? Are you expected to adopt the family code even it conflicts with your sense of integrity and honesty?

Consider also the expectations that family members will have for you. When you have a moment, visit with your hosts and ask what you can do to help, what their expectations are for guests in their home. Are you expected to help clean up after dinner? Change the sheets before you leave after you have stayed with them? Bring a gift every time you visit? Leave a tip for the family housekeeper? Plan and execute a family dinner or holiday meal?

If you have issues with your mate's family and how they treat the two of you, wait to discuss it once you've returned home and had a chance to think about how to bring it up in a constructive, loving fashion. Remember to use "I" statements to express how you felt in a certain situation. The very same issues that bother you may also bother your mate, and to jump all over it right after leaving a family dinner will only make your mate more sensitive and cause him or her to respond irrationally, hurting your relationship. Wait for a more relaxed moment to bring up the fact that Uncle Bruce addressed you as "little girl" rather than calling you by your name. Or that the two of you ended up washing all the pots, pans, dishes, and silverware for a table of twelve by yourself after Thanksgiving dinner, without help and without anyone saying "thank you." Find ways to say "I was hurt by something that was said" or "I felt insulted when she interrupted me or called me a name."

rather than saying "She made me mad when she said...when she called me...when she interrupted me."

Your beloved cannot control his or her family or friends. Keep that in mind as you look to the future and consider how much time you want to spend with the family and how much time you want to spend alone together or with others.

Focus: Know what you are getting into with your beloved's family. Learn what will be expected of you once you are married. Adjust accordingly to create harmony in your relationship together.

Day Five
Your Own Friends

Just like your family of origin, you come with your own coterie of friends. Some may have known you since you were born, others since high school, some from college, others from work. As you grow and change your friends will move in and out of your life. Friends can have their own agendas, their own selfish designs on your time, and their own likes and dislikes of your choice in a lifelong partner. People may work to sabotage their best friends' marriages because they are jealous. They may keep friends out too late, get them drunk, and introduce them to other attractive women and/or men, intending to create enough friction in a marriage to end it.

With social media, it may be easier to keep up with acquaintances, but true friendships will require work and attention. Just like a lovely garden, friendships require nurturing, pruning, time, and attention for growth and maintenance. Every person needs something different. You may have one friend who needs a one-on-one personal visit, or another just a long visit on the phone; still another may want a birthday card or a gift of remembrance. Friends can require a financial investment as well, especially if an expensive lunch, tickets to a show, a nice gift, or traveling to visit is required. Make sure you have a place in your spending plan for your friends.

If you choose to have children, the parents of your children's friends will become your friends. My mother's best friend called it the "brotherhood of motherhood." Through that "brotherhood" a mother learns what is happening at school, what the latest trends are, the dangers lurking in the schoolyard, and what peer pressures concern other mothers.

A good friend once told me that to enhance friendships, you can remember when you first met your friends, send them energy, pray for them, call them, drop them a note, break bread with them, make time for them, and be a good friend to yourself.

True friends have your best interests at heart, maintaining confidences and listening with an open mind and heart. Although you may want someone else to make your decisions for you and help you with the tough times in your life, you will be the one who must solve your own problems and make your own decisions. No one can fix your life but you.

Focus: Your friends will change as you change. A few true friends are a treasure for anyone. Remember to be a friend to yourself as well as to others.

Day Six
A Family of Your Own

A big part of most courting rituals is discussing the imaginary life of the future. Imagine the white picket fence surrounding the two-story house with the front porch and the rocking chairs, along with the 2.5 children, the family dog and a sport utility wagon in the driveway, is the way the conversation may go, but maybe not for you or for your future mate. The family you imagine and the way you want to live is worth a conversation or two before you tie the knot or formalize your relationship.

After a few dates, find out whether your target partner has any children he or she is responsible for financially and physically. If so, ask yourself whether you are willing to care for those children and be responsible for them as if they were your own. Find out their ages, where they live, and who cares for them on a regular basis. If neither of you has children, then start talking about something simple, like pets.

Are you going to have pets? What kind? Will they live in the house or outside? Who will feed them, water them, take them to the vet, and keep them and their living area clean? What will you do with them when you have to be away from home for business or pleasure? What happens if you don't want them anymore? Will you give them to a friend, ask your family to care for them, or leave them at the local animal shelter?

Do you want children? If so, how many? What if you can't procreate because you or your mate are infertile: will you adopt, or will you skip children altogether? How far will you go to deal with the infertility issue? Will you accept your circumstance and learn to live with it and move forward?

Children are not returnable, nor are they commonly put up for adoption unless abuse or neglect are involved, so making sure you really want children and all the work involved with raising them is important. Children require love, and if you are lucky they may give you love, but that is not always the case. You may not get along with your children, and you may not even like your children. They are not pets, and they may not obey you. Hope they respect you and love you just a bit.

A child must be fed, cleaned, dressed, driven to school, taken to the doctor, delivered to after-school activities, and cared for and loved, so make sure you are willing to do all of that, as well as pay for all of the child's other needs. According to

U.S.D.A. research, before a child reaches eighteen years of age it costs an average of at least $241,000 for expenses like clothing, education, child-care, and medical care, not including private school. This does not include the bill for the mother's prenatal care, the delivery of the baby, or any extraordinary medical care a premature infant may require. Children are expensive, so plan accordingly.

Once you have children, who is going to be the primary caregiver? Are you hiring a nanny or using daycare? Will one of you stay at home to care for your children while the other earns the family's main income? Will you take advantage of whatever parental leave your company offers and switch off from one to the other? How traditional are your respective views on childrearing?

How will you discipline your children? Will you only say no, or will you give your child a reason not to do something? Will you employ corporal punishment, spanking or hitting your child? Will you use time-outs as a means of punishment? Will you reward good behavior, and if so, how will you do that? If your first "child" is a dog, you will learn about methods of discipline and your ability to stick to those methods. The results will speak for themselves.

As part of your spending plan and budgeting, you may want to decide whether your children will be attending public schools or private ones. Include tuition, books, and uniforms, as well as special after-school activities, in your financial planning. Will you set up a college savings account for your child so they have money for tuition or room and board when the time comes to get a college degree? Even if they decide to follow a career path that does not require a college degree, training programs that develop employable skills will still be expensive, requiring some savings. Will you expect your children to work while going to school or to earn a scholarship or take on debt to pay their way?

Focus: Before you become a parent, be aware of the financial costs of parenting. Saving money and knowing your partner better before having children will assist you in creating a more stable family.

Day Seven

"Life is what happens to you when you are making other plans"

No one really knows how their life is going to turn out. Discussing your dreams and the life you imagine with the partner you want to spend the rest of your life with gives you a foundation from which to work. You can learn which dreams you share and which you don't. You can figure out how you can save money and what you want to save it for before you are in the middle of the ocean of your life together. You can act in concert together to accomplish shared goals, as opposed to working against each other and your shared desires.

When the unexpected happens, hopefully you will have a nest egg and a little safety net (remember the nest egg of one thousand dollars, and the six to nine months worth of expenses you've saved) to help you through it financially. If you've worked hard on your relationship, then maybe you've built a relationship of love that will give you comfort and security to get you through the crisis you are facing together. Getting to know each other before you get engaged, before you start planning a wedding, before you have children, before you buy a house, is crucial to having a long-term successful relationship. Take your time; don't rush; pay attention to the signs on the highway that urge you to slow down, be careful, and watch where you are going.

Focus: When you look back on a relationship that failed, it is easy to see all the warning signs. Take the time to allow your relationship to blossom and to get to know many, many things about each other before you make a lifelong commitment.

Before the Wedding

1.   Share your spiritual background and beliefs with your beloved. Discuss how these beliefs will be a part of your life together.

2.   Treat your partner with respect and love. Be polite, kind, and loving with each other for the duration of your relationship.

3.   Use loving notes and cards to further express your love to your mate.

4.   Share your sexual expectations with your partner. Work together to find a way to meet each of

your emotional and sexual needs.

5. Share and discuss your health histories with each other. Discuss the role of alcohol, recreational drugs, tobacco, and other substances in your life.

6. Remember that you marry the person and their family and friends. If you have difficulty accepting these people and getting along with them, consider reevaluating the potential success of the relationship.

7. Discuss how much time you will spend with family and friends in your life together.

8. Share your thoughts about children and pets. How will you care for children and pets if you have them? Will you share all the responsibilities for child-care? What will you do if you or your mate is infertile?

9. Remember that planning is designed to make your life less chaotic in the event of a crisis or emergency. Your nest egg and emergency expense savings will carry you through difficult financial times, while your emotional investment in your relationship will hopefully provide stability when times are tough.

Week Ten: Getting Married

No doubt you have the picture-perfect wedding fantasy firmly planted in your head. Movies are made, articles are written, stories are told about the adventures of planning a wedding. You've fallen in love, and you have discussed finances, health, sex, religion, family, and your expectations for each other in your day-to-day lives, now you're ready to get married. Marriage is a legal declaration to the world that you are a partnership facing the world together. You can choose how you want to get married and how splashy a presentation to the world you can afford. With so many decisions to make, the process will give you insight into the kind of life you will have together. If you can't survive the wedding planning, then you may not be able to survive the marriage.

Focus: Your life during the planning of the wedding may be a peek into your life after marriage. Pushy in-laws, demanding brides, tightwad grooms, and passive-aggressive friends may show their true colors during the process. Watch for signs on the road that the bridge may be out further down the highway.

Day One
Rock or No Rock?

Engagement rings have been around for hundreds of years. Ad campaigns for diamonds will tell you they are symbolic of your love for your beloved, with the intimation that a larger diamond indicates a bigger love. Some families pass Granny's diamond down from one generation to another, sometimes with embellishments along the way. Diamonds are known for their strength, which makes them a powerful symbol of the bond between two people. Traditionalists view the engagement ring as an indication of the willingness of the male or dominant partner to provide for his or her beloved, with the value of the stone, and the ring itself, serving as a financial pledge to the couple's future. Some couples choose to do without an engagement ring, allowing a simple band at the wedding ceremony to stand alone as a symbol of their love for each other.

Whatever you and your mate choose, consider some simple math. An engagement ring traditionally costs about two to three times the monthly salary of the purchaser. You don't want to spend the rest of your life paying for the ring. If you want a bigger stone or more diamonds later on in life, then another stone can be purchased or anniversary bands added to commemorate important anniversaries. The original stone can be incorporated into the new setting, or the original sentiment can be preserved in another piece of jewelry. Don't mortgage your future to buy a bigger ring if you cannot afford it. Keep in mind that the ring is considered a gift to the bride-to-be, a gift she or he can keep even if the marriage does not happen, or if it ends in divorce. When the time comes, save money in advance, and pay for the ring in full.

Beyond the family traditions and the advertising media's desire for you to have an engagement ring, there is the question of whether it will be worn at all. Everyone's lifestyle is different. Make a choice together about buying or not buying an engagement ring. If you decide to surprise your mate with a proposal and a ring, then don't be upset if she or he doesn't like the ring or, worse, turns down your marriage proposal. Once you get a positive answer to the question "Will you marry me?" then go out together to find the perfect ring.

Focus: Consider your beloved's taste and preferences, family traditions, and your financial means in choosing whether or not to have an engagement ring.

Day Two
Money during Marriage

Talk about money before you marry. Know the amount of debt belonging to each of you. Find out if you have savings, retirement plans, or other investments. Discuss how financial decisions will be made, who will be responsible for paying the bills, and how you will make major purchases for your household. Map out a budget beforehand with the financial details of how you plan to live together.

Clarify whether you both will be employed and responsible for contributing to the common household coffers and how you together will handle events like childrearing, losing a job, or a serious illness.

Make an agreement to set up a quarterly "State of Our Union" meeting to talk about money and other issues that are relevant to your current life and your future together. Follow up the meeting with a nice dinner or lunch that allows you to make the event a special something you both look forward to instead of dread. Make sure both of you are up-to-date on the status of your income, investments, debt payments, credit card debt, and other aspects of your financial plan. In the event of your death, your partner will be able to carry on during a very difficult time because of the knowledge the two of you share in these meetings.

Avoid the practice where one of you takes care of the finances all the time. Take turns paying bills, filing statements, and tracking expenses so both of you know what is involved and can handle the books when necessary. Having a second set of eyes on the financial aspects of your life together can help you spot trouble areas ahead of time, often enabling you to avoid catastrophes.

Part of your financial planning may include a "Vacation Fund" where you regularly put aside money you can use to pay expenses for a much-needed break in your daily routine. Even a few dollars a day will pay for a nice hotel room and short road trip to a different destination from the one you are living in day in and day out. New scenery and a new environment, even for a few days, can enhance your personal life together, as well as your performance at work.

Focus: If you can't talk about money before you are married, you will probably not be able to talk about it afterward. Marriage is hard work; talking about money is too. Make the effort to do it for each other out of your love for one another and your hope for your future together.

Day Three
Prenuptial Agreements

When billionaires get divorced, the biggest news is about the "prenup" and how much each party is entitled to when the assets accumulated during marriage are divided between the parties. Hopefully your marriage will last forever, but in case it does not, you may want to consider a prenuptial agreement.

Some people say that having a prenup shows pessimism about the likelihood that a marriage will be successful. A woman I know said she feels the prenup is essential because everyone has to share their financial situation honestly, including debts as well as assets. Her attitude is that it starts the couple out being honest with each other about where they are starting their relationship financially and usually requires a discussion about money that might not take place without the process involved in writing the prenuptial agreement. Additionally, a properly drafted agreement can provide protection from your beloved's creditors who might be looking for funds from you. By clearly stating what belongs to whom before you are married, as well as how you define separate or community income, you also clarify what is fair game for bill collectors.

In some states, both parties must have their own legal representation in the drafting of the agreement. For it to be enforceable, some states require that work on the prenuptial agreement begin before any save-the-date cards or information about the wedding date is sent out to prospective guests. In addition, there are legal jurisdictions requiring that the prenuptial agreement be executed and signed before the wedding invitations are mailed in order for the prenup to be enforceable. Once you answer that all-important question "Will you marry me?" discussion of a prenuptial agreement needs to begin.

Make sure you understand your state's laws regarding separate and community property. In some states, separate property is anything you owned separately before you were married. Community property is often any property acquired during marriage. There are exceptions in the law regarding gifts, property purchased with separate property funds, and income from separate property. While you are working on your prenuptial agreement, ask questions to clarify how your state perceives the difference and the establishment of separate versus community property.

If you are afraid to bring up the rational discussion of both your current financial situations because you are concerned that your beloved will react negatively, don't be put off from this task. You will both know more about each other after the discussion than before. If you do get a negative reaction, then ask why. If money is a sensitive subject before you marry, it will only be worse afterward.

Focus: Know your individual and joint financial situation before you marry. Evaluate your options about how you want to treat your assets during your marriage and in the event of a divorce. Seek legal advice as to what is best for you.

Day Four
What Do You Want to Remember Most about Your Wedding?

Considering that the wedding ceremony itself lasts about thirty minutes, at the most an hour, and that most receptions last from three to five hours, the entire event encompasses approximately six hours at the most. You will be so busy socializing that it may be one big blur when you take time to recall it. Of those six hours, what do you most want to remember?

An entire industry is dedicated to the minute details of weddings: the dress, the flowers, the favors, the food, the drink, the linens, the plates, the silverware, the tables, the chairs, the tents, the photographs, the music, the invitations, the save-the-date cards, the invitation list, the gifts, the responses, the transportation, and the wedding party and its attire. The list goes on and on. Of all these details, what will you remember about your wedding? And what do you want to remember about your wedding? It may matter to you to have a photo with Great-grandmother Ruthie, but you may not care if the plates at the table are white with a gold band or just plain white china.

You may want to look beautiful in your dress or handsome in your suit or tuxedo, but will you remember whether the linens have white-on-white embroidery or are standard white tablecloths? Once you decide what matters to you, then go with it. Don't worry about impressing anyone but you and your beloved.

The father of a recent bride told me that the most successful weddings have loving family and friends in attendance, good food, good drink, and good music. Everything else really doesn't matter. Invite the people who matter to you, serve food and beverages you like, and listen to music that makes you happy.

Focus: It is your wedding. Please yourselves within your financial means.

Day Five
Paying for the Wedding

Whether the ceremony and reception will be attended by the two of you alone or by entertaining every person you know, consider the cost of what you are doing in relation to the enjoyment you are receiving. Make decisions based on what pleases the two of you. A small wedding followed by a great honeymoon; the two of you on a beach with your closest friends; a ceremony at a small chapel in the country with a picnic afterward; an outdoor service in a garden with champagne and cake afterward: weddings come in every shape and size, so make it memorable and special for you.

Remember to be considerate of whoever is paying for your wedding. Is your family traditional, living with the belief that the ceremony and reception are the financial responsibility of the bride's family, while the groom and his family take care of the rehearsal dinner? Or are you and your partner going to pay your own way for this special event?

Be considerate of your family and their ability to pay. Ask how much they are willing to spend or plan to spend. If you and your partner are paying for everything yourselves, then venture carefully into the discussion of your idea of a dream wedding. Wedding expenses can mount up quickly and usually the more frills you have and the more people you invite, the more you will spend.

Be careful about spending more than you can afford. Going into debt in order to pay for an event that lasts less than a day may not be in your best interests. Work out a wedding plan that respects a budget and gives you what your heart desires.

Focus: Be considerate of your parents, your future in-laws, and your budget when planning your wedding.

Day Six

Wedding Expenses

Before you set your heart on your perfect wedding, think about these numbers. A destination wedding can cost upward of $60,000. Entertaining three hundred of your closest friends with a band, dinner, and open bar will run at least $100,000. Sharing your joy with immediate family and friends with wedding cake and domestic champagne and a four-piece band may run around $10,000 or more. If you imagined the type of wedding featured in the magazines and on television, now you may want to think about having a small wedding and spending your money on a great honeymoon instead.

Will you need a wedding planner? A professional can help you from the date you are engaged through the stroke of midnight the day you are married. If you don't need that much help, then hire a planner just for the day of the wedding to take care of the details that you don't have time to attend to on your special day. If you can't afford a planner, then perhaps a trusted friend will agree to handle the details on the day of the ceremony and receptions. Obviously, you will have to have some kind of organized system in place so you can delegate all the tasks on the schedule, as well as the phone numbers for the limo, florist, musicians, cake maker, caterer, wedding party, and anyone else needed for your ceremony and reception. Find a wedding planner who understands the concept of a budget and staying within that budget. Some wedding planners both charge you a fee and receive commissions from the various vendors recommended to you. Inquire about how the planners you are interviewing are paid, read their contract, and verify their references.

Based on personal experience, here's a list of typical wedding expenses you may encounter along the journey to your special day. Once you research the range of costs for each category, you can create a spending plan that fits your financial situation or that of your family. Congratulations on your upcoming nuptials, and good luck!

1. Location for the ceremony
2. Wedding license
3. Honorarium for the officiate (minister or judge)

4. Clothing for the happy couple (wedding dress? new suit or tux rental?)

5. Flowers (bouquet, boutonnières, the ceremony location, the reception location)

6. Photographer (engagement photo, bridal portrait, ceremony, reception)

7. Videographer (during the ceremony and the reception)

8. Transportation for the wedding party

9. Transportation for wedding guests (out-of-town guests)

10. Save-the-date cards

11. Invitations and response cards, including postage for both

12. Reception location

13. Reception decorations

14. Beverages at the reception

15. Food at the reception

16. Music at the ceremony and the reception

17. Party favors

18. Gifts for the wedding party (bridesmaids and groomsmen)

19. Valet parking

20. Hotel rooms (first night of marriage)

21. Tips for everyone

22. Stationery for thank-you notes

23. Activities for children if they are invited (babysitter?)

24. Future wedding gifts you will have to give to all the people not yet married whom you invited to your wedding

25. Wedding planner (if you need one)

Focus: Decide what you want to spend on your wedding, then create your spending plan, including only the items you need. Take pleasure in creating a beautiful day with elegance and style while spending within your means.

Day Seven
After the Wedding

Once the music stops, the cake is gone, the champagne bottles are empty, and your friends and family have returned home, you and your betrothed will be married. Together you will face the world and all its challenges. Don't be surprised if you feel a little emotional letdown after all the planning and excitement of executing your wedding. Your honeymoon is the opportunity for you and your mate to take a vacation to recover from your wedding and settle into life together.

Hopefully you've been as careful in developing the spending plan for your honeymoon trip as for your wedding. Setting money aside for a destination that fits your overall spending plan will make your return to married life together more pleasant. Taking a road trip to a small country inn or a quaint seaside village or to a glossy hotel in a nearby city will be a great beginning to life together. If you have airline miles from business trips you've taken, then book a flight to an exotic locale as the foundation for a trip abroad. Consider your accommodations and your meals, as well as transportation around your destination, when you are figuring out your honeymoon trip. If you can't afford to travel out of town, then stay at a hotel or inn nearby, and don't tell anyone where you will be. Explore your hometown like a tourist: see the sights, take long naps, go out for dinner and dancing.

Once you get to your romantic destination, remember it is the time you spend together that will be memorable. Take long walks together, enjoy a picnic lunch, and partake in free entertainment that the locals enjoy. Rest and relax from the excitement and exhaustion of your wedding and your everyday life.

Back from your honeymoon, savor the first year of marital life. Whether you lived together before marriage or not, expect a little turbulence with the change of status. Usually there is a power struggle during the first year, with conflicted discussions about everything from who takes out the trash to how much money each of you spent the previous month. Don't be surprised if one of you seems to "change." Be your loving self and calmly speak up about how you feel about how your relationship is going. Remember that marriage requires clear communication, honesty, respect for one another, and work.

Be happy you found someone you love and with whom you want to live forever. Remember to tell each other "I love you!" at least once a day. Greet each other on returning home with a kiss and welcome embrace. Remember birthdays and anniversaries with a memento of some kind: a card, a gift, some flowers or a note. Listen to each other more, and talk less. A marriage is a friendship; it takes nurturing, listening, attention, and thinking of your beloved's interest as well as your own.

Focus: Now that you are married, be thoughtful toward each other and continue to work on the relationship and your expectations for the future.

Getting Married

1.   Planning the wedding may be a preview of your life together after marriage.

2.   An engagement ring may or may not be necessary for you. Discuss it with each other openly and honestly. Spend about two to three times your monthly salary for the purchase of the ring.

3.   If you can't talk about money before marriage, you will only argue about it afterward. Work out a budget to figure out how much you will be able to save and spend once you are married.

4.   If you plan to have a prenuptial agreement, then draft and execute it before everyone is notified of the wedding through save-the-date cards and wedding invitations.

5.   Be considerate of your parents, in-laws, and your budget when planning your wedding ceremony and reception.

6.   Know what you really need to create your beautiful, elegant, special wedding day, and set your budget accordingly.

7.   Enjoy a honeymoon that respects your financial situation. Do not go into debt to pay for your wedding or your honeymoon.

Wedding Budget Worksheet

Wedding Expense Plan

	Budget	Actual	Difference
Location for the ceremony			
Wedding license			
Honorarium for the officiate			
Clothing for the happy couple			
Flowers			
Photographer			
Videographer			
Transportation for the wedding party			
Transportation for wedding guests			
Save-the-date cards			
Invitations and response cards			
Postage for invitations/cards			
Reception location			
Reception decorations			
Beverages at the reception			
Food at the reception			
Music at the ceremony and at the reception			
Party-favors			
Gifts for the wedding party			
Valet parking			

Hotel rooms

Tips for everyone

Stationery for thank-you notes

Activities for children if they are invited

Future wedding gifts you will have to give

Wedding planner

Total Expenses

Week Eleven: Buying a Home

After marriage, buying a home is the biggest commitment you will make in your life. You will commit money, time, furnishings, plants, art, and energy to your home with the hopes that you will get what you expect from it. You may live in the first home you buy all of your adult life, or you may move every three to five years, (the national average), going to a different location because of your job or your family.

For many people their home is their base camp, the place they come to when they need to feel comforted and safe. For others it's just a place to change clothes and sleep. Knowing what you are looking for in a home will make it easier for you to select a place that meets your needs, fits in your spending plan, and gives you a reasonable return on your investment.

Of course you can always sell your home, but it may not take as little time as you hope, especially if you forget to follow some basic rules when you are making that important decision.

Day One

Location, Location, Location

The three key words in real estate are location, location, location. The most important feature of the property you plan to buy is the location. Will it be in a safe neighborhood? Is it in a good school district? How close are a grocery store, pharmacy, restaurant, dry cleaner, laundry, gas station, important employers, and major thoroughfares? Is it in a place where houses sell quickly? Have property values been increasing in this area? You want to buy a home in the best location you can afford so that it is more likely to maintain its value through the years you live in it.

Once you figure out the best locations for you, evaluate the different types of developments in those locations. Do you want to live in a condominium complex, own a townhouse, live in a high-rise, or have your own yard? Your specific needs, your budget, and how much free time you have available may determine what is best for you. If you imagine your own garden and a yard for your dog Rex to run in, then consider the added responsibility of keeping the yard, whether you do it yourself, or pay a service to care for it. If you are away on business a great deal of the time, a condominium complex or high-rise might be best for you, with someone else maintaining the grounds, taking care of maintenance for you, and securing the common areas. If you want more than a condo or townhouse, but less to care for than a house, consider a house with limited patio space or a garden home.

Keep in mind that you may live in this dwelling for a long time, so think about how it will work for you over time. Will it accommodate a spouse if you choose to marry, or a family if you have children? Will you be willing to have a roommate or two if you need the income to help with the mortgage, or is this a place you want all to yourself until your life changes dramatically?

Focus: Determine your expectations for the home you are going to buy. Select the perfect location taking into account those expectations and then figure out what kind of personal investment you are willing to make.

Day Two

What Can You Afford to Pay?

A lot of factors go into figuring out what you will be willing to pay for a home. Before you go much further, consider that you may want to limit your monthly mortgage payment to about twenty-five percent of your take-home pay. If you are taking home $3,000 a month, then you can afford a mortgage payment of $750 per month. You can spend more if you like, but it will affect your ability to do other things, because more of your money will be going toward your house. Get a fixed-rate mortgage, not a floating-rate one. Also, avoid mortgages that have a fixed rate for a short period of time and then become a floating-rate mortgage or have a bump-up clause where the rate goes up automatically.

During the 2008 global financial crisis, mortgages that had these bump-up clauses in place ruined peoples' lives. Many had mortgages that were at a four percent fixed rate that then jumped to a nine percent mortgage rate after the first five-year period at a fixed rate expired. Most of these people originally thought they were going to get a thirty-year mortgage with a five percent fixed rate, but when they went to sign the documents, they were tempted into agreeing to a thirty-year mortgage with a lower rate of four percent, which lowers the monthly payments. However, that rate was only good for five years rather than the full thirty years, leading to devastating circumstances for people who did not read the fine print. Carefully reading the documents would have prevented some of these problems that surprised consumers who went with the lower rate, not understanding that it was not the same type of loan.

More than the mortgage amount, there are other expenses associated with the residence you are looking to buy. Electric, gas, water, sewer, garbage collection, Home Owner's Association (HOA) dues, insurance, taxes, Internet, phone, security, and yard and pool maintenance are all extra fees that each month are part of the cost of owning your own home. In some instances, non-payment or late payment of HOA dues can result in your home being foreclosed on by the Home Owner's Association. Carefully read the bylaws of any HOA before you finalize your purchase.

Focus: Figure out how much you can afford to spend on your home each month, and then look for properties in the price range of the mortgage you can afford.

Day Three
Can You Get a Mortgage?

Now that you have determined what you are comfortable spending each month on your home purchase, consider the requirements for applying for a mortgage and making an offer on a property for sale. Most lenders require a ten percent to twenty percent down payment on the purchase of a house, condo, or townhouse, depending on your credit score. If you are looking to buy something for $100,000, then be prepared to pay $10,000 to $20,000 as the down payment, with a loan amount of the remaining $90,000 or $80,000. The down payment becomes the equity in your home.

In addition to the money for the down payment, you may have to pay for a survey of the property, a title policy, which is insurance that the title to the land is good and there are no liens on the real estate or house, and possibly a commission to the real estate sales person who listed the house or who is representing you in the transaction. It is also wise to have a real estate attorney look over the documents before you sign to verify their proper execution.

Lenders also require proof of income, often requesting copies of tax returns for the previous two or three years, copies of bank and brokerage statements, W2 forms, 1099 statements, and paystubs if applicable. Usually the application will require that you list any assets and debts you have and then require that you provide backup documentation.

When looking for a mortgage you may wish to contact your banker, accountant, lawyer, investment advisor, insurance agent, and any friends for recommendations about mortgage sources. Your real estate agent may also have contacts with a mortgage broker or banker who can help you through the application process. Your credit score will be a big part of what determines your eligibility for different lenders as well as the interest rate available to you when you make your purchase. Beware of a mortgage that requires a higher monthly payment than you can afford. Do not assume that the financial professional preparing the documents knows anything about what is right for your personal financial situation.

Focus: Getting a mortgage involves your credit score, a down payment funded by your personal savings and investments, and proof of a steady stream of income.

Day Four

What Other Expenses Are Involved in Owning a Home?

Besides the mortgage payment each month, there will be other maintenance expenses that will keep your house in good working order and make it a comfortable place to be. Obviously you will pay electric bills to keep the lights on, water bills for health and hygiene, gas to cook with or heat your home, and heating oil or coal if you live in colder climates, but there are additional fees to include in your expense plan for comfort, pleasure, and safety.

As you look at different homes, keep in mind the age and maintenance of the appliances and the heating and air-conditioning equipment in the home you are buying. Once it's yours, then you will be responsible for maintaining it or replacing it. Heating and air-conditioning equipment should be serviced two times per year, usually in late spring for the air conditioner, and then late fall for the heater. Dryer vents and chimneys should be cleaned every two years to prevent fires. Various appliances such as refrigerators, ovens, dishwashers, washers, and dryers will have to be serviced when they malfunction. Toilets and sinks can back up and overflow, and faucets can leak, requiring plumbing work. Many sellers include a whole-house insurance policy to cover the appliances and air-handling systems for a specified limited time period when offering their homes for sale.

Keeping your home clean to maintain it over the years takes time and cleaning supplies. Whether you clean it yourself, or hire someone to do so, keeping your home clean maintains its value, helping you later when you sell it. Sometimes areas that need paint, repair, or replacement can be spotted earlier if a house is kept clean and neat.

If you have a yard or patio, it may require regular care. Whether it needs mowing, trimming, weeding, sweeping, planting, or watering, take into account the cost of the supplies, time, and employees involved in that maintenance. If you are too busy to do the work yourself, you may need to hire someone to do it, as many communities have laws about yard maintenance and cleanup.

With the development of more and more gated communities or limited-access communities, as well as condos and high-rises, there are more homeowner's association dues paid than ever before. Many of these associations include a clause in their bylaws allowing foreclosure on properties when the dues are not paid in a timely fashion or are in arrears for several months. If you make an offer on a home covered by a homeowner's association, make sure you receive, read, and understand a copy of the bylaws before the end of the opt-out period for your offer.

Insurance and taxes are the two biggest expenses you will pay outside of your mortgage. Property tax in many communities usually pays for police and fire protection, improvements to the water and sewer systems, school systems, public hospitals, and road and street improvements. Insurance can cover your home in the event of fire, some types of water damage, theft, and other damage. Your policy will tell you what is and what is not covered. Almost all lenders require basic insurance on the dwelling, but not the contents.

If you decide to buy an older home or one that requires a lot of work, it may be worthwhile to make a list, in order of priority, of the work that needs to be done, and then get a bid from a contractor as to the cost of making those improvements before you make an offer. Having that information can help you make an offer that is appropriate for the dwelling you are considering as well as provide a bargaining point during the offer and counter-offer period. It may also help you decide between one place or another based on the actual after-purchase cost with the improvements included.

Focus: Be aware of extra expenses involved in owning a home, over and above your mortgage, before you make the purchase of a home.

Day Five
Can You Insure the Home of Your Dreams?

Knowing what the insurance on the structure will cost will help you in your spending plan for your home, as well as your overall budget. Factor these figures into your planning and take the time to go over the terms of the insurance policy with your agent. There are liability limits for the structure, personal property, and general liability associated with the policy. Also, there is a deductible----that is, the amount you will have to pay out of your own pocket before the insurance chips in for the remainder. Remember, an insurance policy is a bet between you and the insurance company. You are betting there will be a problem, and the insurance company is betting there won't be, or if there is one, it won't happen often. You are paying each month so that if something happens to your house, then the insurance company will step forward and make a payment toward the damages. If nothing happens, and you do not make a claim, then the insurance company keeps your monthly payments.

Not all homes can be insured against fire, flood, or windstorm damage. Before you make the offer for the home you want, check with your insurance agent to find out whether the property is insurable. If you don't have an agent, ask friends, family, or knowledgeable professionals for referrals to trusted insurance agents who can help you before you buy.

Your insurance agent may discover there was a previous claim for damage on the property a few years before, alerting you to the need to inquire about that damage and the cleanup afterward. It may also remind you to look closely for any other damage and ask about any insurance claims, as well.

Properties located in coastal areas may require windstorm insurance, which may be very expensive and difficult to purchase. Flood insurance may be advisable if you are looking at purchasing land near the 500-year or 100-year flood plain. Flood plain maps are updated every ten years or so and are available online if you want to find out where flooding risk may be more likely to occur.

If you are looking to purchase a condominium or a townhouse, verify that the buildings comply both with your lender's requirements and with your insurance company's. In the last few years, cities have started building certification programs that verify the compliance of a structure with the local building codes and safety requirements. Check with both your lender and your insurance agent to make sure your dream home fits within their criteria.

Focus: Before making an offer, get an insurance quote from your agent and verify that the property fits within your lender's and your insurance company's guidelines.

Day Six

What Happens if I Want to Sell It?

Your life can change in the blink of an eye. One minute you are single; the next you are married. Children may become a part of your life. You may decide you want a dog that needs a yard. An ailing parent may come live with you. A new job may require that you move to another location. For these reasons and more, at some point you may choose to sell your home.

Resale value can be influenced by a great number of factors, but the most important is location, location, location. If the economy is stable or booming in the city where you live, there will be other people moving there for jobs. If businesses are leaving the area, then there will be more houses for sale, and fewer people to buy them. Beyond the economy, the part of town you live in, along with its popularity among all age groups, can enhance the resale value of your home. Does your particular house appeal to all age groups? Are there too many stairs that will cause older people to shun your house? Is the yard big enough for children and pets to play in, but not so large that it requires a full-time gardener? The more people your house will appeal to, the better chance you will have to sell it quickly.

When realtors ask you to de-clutter your house, put away personal pictures and mementos, and "stage" your house, they are using psychology to make sure your house appeals to more people. A buyer may have an idea of what they are looking for, but you have to make sure your house "looks" and "smells" like the great house everyone wants to live in. To sell your house it must appear to be comfortable, clean, and perfect to fulfill the buyer's fantasy of their dream house.

If your house is the largest house on the block or the largest in the neighborhood you live in, it may not sell as quickly as smaller houses in the same area. Again, that is because there are fewer prospects for the larger houses. More people can afford the smaller house down the block, so there will be greater interest in that property. Before you buy your home, keep the end in mind: think about how easy or hard it will be to sell the house you are considering buying.

When you are looking at buying a house, consider the number of days a house has been on the market. The longer the number of days, the more motivated the seller. It also tells you that there may be something about the house----its location, floor plan, yard, or neighborhood----that makes it less appealing than others. Realtors can fudge those numbers as well by listing a house for three months, taking it off the market for a week, and then listing it again for three months. Using that technique makes the house a "new" listing every ninety days, possibly obscuring the fact it may have been on the market for over a year before you saw it or before it sold.

Focus: When buying a home, keep the end in mind. Think about the process of reselling the property in the future.

Day Seven
Is this House a Good Investment?

The value of residential real estate fluctuates with the economy. If interest rates are low, banks have money to lend on homes, and if a community is flourishing, then residential real estate will most likely go up in value. But before you decide you are going to become the king or queen of flipping real estate, remember that you'll be lucky if you can buy a home, live in it for years, and then sell it for what you paid for it. With mortgage interest deductions from your income taxes, as well as property tax deductions currently allowed by the tax law, you will be living rent free, and hopefully keeping the money you invested in the house in the first place.

If the economy goes against you, you may find that you are underwater, meaning the house is worth less than the mortgage amount remaining to be paid. It happened in 2008 all over the country, and it happened in Texas in the early 1980s after the oil boom went bust and the banks and savings and loans that lent money on anything with the word "oil" in it went into receivership. So it can happen again. Prepare for it by making a decent down payment, working to pay off your mortgage as quickly as you can, and not overreaching on the mortgage, taking on more debt than you can afford.

When you evaluate whether this home of your dreams will be a good investment, consider the surrounding area. Is this home in a new development where there will be lots of new homes built around it, all competing for buyers? Or is it located in an established part of town where the neighborhoods are fairly stable with good schools and a well-woven net of community involvement? Will the demand for housing in the area where your dream home is located continue? Is it close to where the jobs are? Will living there shorten the commute to work for you, as well as others? Is it in an up-and-coming part of town? Or is it in an older area enjoying a renaissance? Does everyone want to live in this location? Is the demand for housing in that area likely to continue? If you can answer yes to most of the above questions, then your house may be a good investment.

After you decide to move on to your next abode, will you be able to rent this house, condo, or townhouse and cover a part or all of your basic expenses for that property? If you are buying a condo or townhouse, make sure there are no restrictions about renting to a non-owner. Some condo or townhouse boards reserve the right to approve any buyers or tenants in a building or complex to prevent unsavory types from living in their neighborhood. If you can rent to anyone who can make the rent and who satisfies your background-check criteria, then that may add to the investment potential of your dream house.

Although anything can happen to upset well-thought-out plans, keep in mind that your best source of prospective tenants may come from your neighbors themselves. They may have a friend or a family member who wants to live close by, either by necessity or desire. Your tenant may start out renting and then ultimately want to buy the house, condo, or townhouse after they live there awhile. Some of your neighbors may appreciate learning you are renting or selling before you make that news public in case they know someone they'd like as a neighbor.

If you decide to be a real estate mogul or landlord that lives off the rent checks paid by your tenants, remember to keep maintenance expenses and repair costs in mind as well as the expense of increasing taxes and insurance premiums. Leasing a property to others makes sense only when it makes money for you.

Focus: Every feature that makes a house a good one to live in will be a factor in its investment value. After living in your home for a number of years, you will be lucky if it is worth the same amount as it was the day you bought it.

Buying a Home

1.   Based on your personal expectations for your home, select a location that meets those expectations.

2.   Figure out how much you can afford to spend each month on your mortgage, then consider buying homes in that price range.

3.   When you apply for a mortgage, the lender will take into account your credit score, your personal assets and debts, your income, and your ability to make a down payment.

4.   Be aware of all the other expenses involved in owning a home: taxes, HOA dues, utilities, maintenance, and insurance, as well as others.

5.   Make sure the home you are considering purchasing is eligible for insurance coverage.

6.   Before purchasing a home, evaluate its resale potential.

7.   If you can live in a house for years and sell it for what you paid for it, then it has been a good investment. Make sure you can rent your house, condo, or townhouse to others in case you are unable to sell it.

Week Twelve: Charity in Your Life

Depending on your background, your first experience with giving money to charity, also known as philanthropy, may have started with church on Sunday and dropping money in the collection plate. You may remember the Salvation Army personnel with their bright red kettle at the shopping mall ringing bells as they collected money for the poor at Christmastime. Maybe your family put together a basket of presents for a child whose holiday wishes found their way to a star on the Angel Tree at the mall. Whatever your experience, the gift you made was one that made a difference in your community. Charitable giving is part of the balance everyone needs in life.

Day One

Why Give Back?

Giving back to your community through gifts to charities, churches, the needy and the poor makes your community a better place to live. Even the smallest amount can make a difference if a great number of people give.

Some people give because they are interested in a particular cause. Others give as part of their religious beliefs. Often people give simply because they get a tax write-off for a portion of their gift. Many give in memory of someone important to them or in honor of an individual who inspires them. There are those who give because they want to be remembered long after they have died. A gift to make a difference in just one life happens all the time. A person may give because they feel that but for the grace of God they might find themselves poor, hungry, homeless, or needy in some way.

You have the freedom to give for whatever reason suits you, but please consider including philanthropy and charitable giving in your financial spending plan.   The world will be a better place because of your gifts.

Focus: The more you give, the more you get back. Of those to whom much has been given, much is expected.

Day Two
What Can I Give?

You can give of yourself: your time, your experience, your wisdom, and your intelligence. You can give of your wealth: money, possessions, and specific items you purchase for a charity's wish list. You can give of your love through your tender works for those who need it: babies, children, animals, the poor, the elderly, and the homeless.

At different times of your life you may find that giving money directly to a charity may be the easiest and best thing to do. At other times, you may find that your soul needs the direct contact with other living creatures. When you are first starting out in life, time spent as a volunteer can give you valuable insights as to what type of work you might want to do for your career, and it will give you experience that can help you later on in life.

Never underestimate the power of the person you are. You have unique talents and gifts that you can share. You may not know what they are yet, but give yourself a chance. Don't assume for a minute that just because you do not have any money you do not have anything to give.

Volunteer at your church or synagogue or mosque to care for children during services, offer to walk a dog for a neighbor, spend time at the local homeless shelter, knit scarves and hats for soldiers, make signs for a neighborhood parade or meeting, hand out leaflets about emergency preparedness for the local Red Cross, take food to the local police and fire station over the holidays: there are a myriad of ways that you can give back and serve your community regardless of your financial situation in life.

Focus: Giving of yourself and your talents will enhance your quality of life and that of your community.

Day Three

Charities Are Businesses Too

Even though a charity is often referred to as a not-for-profit or a non-profit, that does not mean they are not a business. Just like any other enterprise, they employ individuals, contract with other businesses, and produce a product or offer a service just like a for-profit business. The difference is that all of the money received, whether given as gifts or earned through business operations, is applied toward the mission of serving others who are in need or who are the beneficiary of the mission as stated by the organization.

If the mission is to provide day care for children who are considered at risk, then any money received as donations, or paid by parents who can afford care, goes to pay for business expenses. These costs include the location where the children are cared for, the employees' salaries, the toys, the cleaning expenses, water, electric and gas, food for the children, playground equipment, and administrative costs, which can include the manager, the computer systems, the clerical employees, and fundraising expenses. Usually non-profit businesses do not pay sales tax, nor do they pay property tax on the property they own and use for the delivery of their mission.

Just like a for-profit business, a charity can be well managed or poorly managed. A charity can be effective in addressing its mission, or it can be ineffective. There are many charities that share the same mission. They may cover different geographic areas or different demographic groups, or may specialize in a particular problem in your community.

Each non-profit, with the exception of religious organizations and non-profits that review charities, is required to file a Form 990, their tax return, with the Internal Revenue Service of the U.S. Treasury, where they clearly state their mission, the salaries paid to their top employees, and the services they provide to their communities. Copies of the Form 990 are available to the public for perusal on the Internet. Information on 1.6 million charities recognized by the IRS are featured on the Guidestar website at www.guidestar.org.

Focus: A non-profit charity is a business too. Learn about how the charity spends its money before you make a contribution to that organization. Make an informed and wise choice about where you give your charitable gifts.

Day Four
To What Organizations Do I Give?

Throughout your life you will be drawn to different charities as your interests change. If you found a lost dog or cat when you were a child, then you may want to give to a charity that helps homeless animals. If a friend of yours is diagnosed with cystic fibrosis, then you may want to give to a charity that does research to find treatment for that disease.

If you belong to a religious organization that promotes tithing, then you may give ten percent of your income to the church or to other charities annually. Your high school or college may receive your support because of your belief in education and your hope that others will benefit from what your alma mater offers. If a local art museum is a haven of peace and beauty for you, you may want to help keep it open through your contributions. Whatever your reason for supporting a particular charity, give to support the charity work that is important to you.

If you find that there are six different charities that are searching for a treatment for a disease, then you may research their work to verify that your gift, your money, your investment in that charity, is going to be used in the best possible way. Take a look at the form 990. Do their expenses seem ordinary and necessary? Are they paying for luxuries with the donations they receive? If so, maybe they don't really need your money. Compare and contrast their expenses with another organization that has a similar mission. You may find that there is one charity that stands out above the rest, truly deserving your gift, or you may discover that there are five different ones all worthy in their pursuit of the same mission. How you give your money is up to you.

In evaluating a charity, look at the administrative costs compared to the overall budget. If over half the money is spent to pay administrative staff versus paying to deliver services, it might be best to look at another candidate or two as your gift recipient. Consider the impact your gift is making.

How many people, children, or animals are being served by your gift? If only a small number is being served, what is the cost per member of the service population? Is that reasonable, or is it outrageous compared to other non-profits? Does their work help the most people, children, or animals? If a specialized service is being provided, the cost per unit served may be higher than it is for other organizations.

Consider how much debt a charity has on its balance sheet. Is there a plan to pay off the debt in a timely fashion? Does the debt expense take away too much money from the delivery of services for the charity's mission? Is there an endowment to provide income to further its mission? Is the organization receiving more charitable gifts each year, or is it getting less and less support from donors? Consider the vitality of the non-profit from the point of view of its growth and ability to serve its community.

A well-managed non-profit has a healthy balance sheet, steady cash flow, and low employee turnover, and maintains its facilities and continues its mission in the community, thriving and growing. Consider the need of those served by the non-profit, rather than the need of the non-profit itself when you make a gift. A well-managed charity may look like it does not "need" the money, but it may need a stable group of regular supporters. Another charity that needs the money could be a start-up or badly managed. Remember, your gift is an investment in that charity; you are a stakeholder in its success and the delivery of its mission.

Focus: Evaluate the non-profit charities to which you give just as you would a company you would invest in. Make sure you are contributing to an organization that is thriving and will continue to thrive and serve your community.

Day Five

Philanthropy as an Economic Generator

Every time you make a gift of time or money, you are keeping a non-profit business going. Whether you give one dollar or a million, that money has a multiplier effect within your community and beyond of five to eight times the value of the gift. That money is spent to pay someone to answer a phone, type a letter, make phone calls, build a building, design a clinic, run a school, teach a class, or whatever it is the people who work for the non-profit charity do. In turn they spend that money too, so it keeps on moving through the community providing work and income for others.

Not only do the dollars you give create more wealth for others; also, the work done by the non-profit charity, whether it is a school, soup kitchen, clinic, or day care center, helps others by providing a needed boost in their lives. Whether someone is getting food to eat, another credit toward graduation, an appointment to see a doctor, or time to go to work free of worry about their child, those gifts and services further the economy now and in the future.

When a capital campaign is completed, an architect draws up the plans; a contractor orchestrates the construction; the subcontractors of electricians, plumbers, air-conditioning and heating technicians install their part of the building; interior designers select the wall colors, furnishings, and floorings; and specialists help with laboratory equipment, computer interfaces and equipment, doors, windows, and other fixtures. Backhoe and bulldozer operators, dump-truck drivers, security guards, and fence contractors, among others, are all part of the symphony at work when a new building is under way. Whether it is the headquarters of a new charity hospital or a building full of classrooms, there are thousands of people who work on the project and are paid to do so.

When those who work for non-profits spend their paycheck, then the grocer, the pharmacist, the telephone repairperson, the dry cleaner, the plumber, the water company employee, the clothing store salesperson, the shoe salesperson, the bakery counter clerk, the barista, and many others earn their salaries, and on and on it goes.

For every dollar or dollar's worth of time you give, it multiplies in your community five to eight times. That means your one-dollar gift becomes five to eight dollars. A charity with a million-dollar budget has a $5 million to $8 million impact on its community. Your gift keeps on giving to others.

Focus: Each gift to a charity has a multiplier of 5 to 8 times in its benefit to your community. Your community is a better place because of your gifts.

Day Six

Sharing Your Interest in Giving

When you feel strongly about a charity and the work that charity does in the community, you may want to share your passion with your family and friends. People do not give of their time and talents naturally; they usually must be taught to give or encouraged or asked to give by someone else. Part of your gift may be to share it with others to encourage them to be involved in a charity through giving their money or their time.

If you give to your local museum because you enjoy the beauty and serenity of being there, you may want to invite a friend or family member to go with you to see an exhibition or a lecture or special event. Tell them about your involvement, whether you are a member or large donor or volunteer your time there. Explain why you like it and how you enjoy being a part of an organization that enhances the quality of life in your community.

When you go to a party or have dinner with friends, your activities or interest in the symphony, the museum, the homeless shelter, the animal shelter, or your alma mater may interest others and inspire them to follow your example. This involvement adds to your life and the lives of others.

If and when you have a family, show your children how to give by example. Include them in putting together a holiday basket for a family in need. Give them money to put in the Salvation Army contribution bucket outside the store during the holidays. When it is their birthday, consider a small gift in their honor to a charity that helps other children or animals, in addition to the usual celebration. As they get older, explain why you give money to charities and help them learn about groups in their city that do good works. Make volunteering a family affair.

Instead of birthday or holiday gifts, consider asking family members to give to a charity of your choice in your honor for that special occasion. Organize an event where the money collected goes to charity while you and your friends have a nice evening or lunch. Host a movie night where everyone brings a can of food that as a group you donate to the local food bank. Step outside your everyday life to make a difference for others.

Focus: Share your passion for a charity with family and friends.

Day Seven
You Can't Take It with You

Hopefully over your lifetime you will enjoy the pleasure of a wonderful mate, happy family, loving friends, fulfilling work, and interesting experiences. Along the way you may accumulate some money, none of which you can take to the world beyond the grave. You may decide to leave whatever you have left to your family and friends, or you may decide you want to benefit them as well as the charities that matter to you during your lifetime.

Most charities will help you develop strategies for leaving money to them and to your family as well, with tax benefits for you and them at the time of your death. Some of these structures can be created in your will, while others may need to be established in anticipation of your death. Be cautious, though. Don't give away the farm or your home assuming you won't need it. If you live longer than you think, or your investments don't work out like you hoped, you just might want to have your home to fall back on later as a source of cash or income.

If you have amassed a great deal of wealth valued in the hundreds of millions or billions, you may want to establish a family foundation that will leave a legacy for years to come. Members of your family or friends or members of your community can serve on the foundation's board, charged with the mission of what you want done with your money after you are gone. Many cities have community foundations with community boards that administer donor-designated funds; the administration of such foundations is often provided at a shared cost to the donor.

Are you interested in education, arts, human services, the environment, science, medicine, or all of the above? Several organizations may be worthy of your giving a significant bequest upon your death. If you find you are in the position of having great wealth and a giving nature, then consult with estate-planning experts, attorneys, and accountants on the strategies that will allow your assets to give to the communities that matter to you.

Focus: You can't take your wealth with you when you die, but you can leave it for the benefit of others. Ask an estate-planning attorney about strategies that will benefit those you love and the charities that matter to you.

Charity in Your Life

1. Make charitable giving a part of your life.

2. Of those to whom much has been given, much is expected.

3. Giving of yourself and your talents will enhance your quality of life and that of your community.

4. Make an informed choice about where you give your wealth and talents.

5. Give to an organization that is thriving and will continue to thrive as it serves your community.

6. Each gift to charity has an economic multiplier effect of 5 to 8: that is, every dollar you give generates five to eight dollars in your community.

7. Share your passion for charity with family and friends.

8. Learn about and use estate-planning strategies that benefit your family and the charities in your community.

Congratulations!

You finished MoneySmarts4U! I hope you have a better understanding about how to use money as a tool to create the life you want. Now that you know more about your relationship with money, you can address the areas where money gives you trouble. Feel free to review the sections of this book that apply to your particular issues with money whenever you need help.

Right now you may not need some of the information in the various readings, but later on this book may be just the source of knowledge you seek. Keep this book handy, reference it when you are faced with a financial decision or life decision unfamiliar to you.

Most of all enjoy the journey of taking over the management of your life and your money. There are so many opportunities for you to have a wonderful life full of growth, love, peace, joy, and prosperity.   Explore it, delight in it, and have fun with it.   You have everything within you to live a successful and happy life.   Remember that taking care of your money is part of taking care of yourself. I know you can do it!

With encouragement,

Barbie

Author's Note and Acknowledgment

For many years I have given seminars, classes, and workshops on money management. After the financial debacle of 2008, so many people, children, families, and lives were destroyed by the collapse of their finances. Determined to do something to help others avoid experiencing this kind of catastrophe in their lives, I started work on the *MoneySmarts4U* concept outline and book. I realized this material needs to be consumed in bite-sized pieces, hence the daily reading format over a short twelve-week period. This is the first of the *MoneySmarts4U* series, *MoneySmarts4U: The Basics*, with *MoneySmarts4U: Investments*, *MoneySmarts4U: Women's Edition*, and *MoneySmarts4U: Retirement* to follow. Hopefully these books will help people make good choices with their money and improve their relationship with the money in their lives.

I want to thank the following people with tremendous gratitude for their encouragement: Janine, for insisting I write this book in time for her daughter, Danielle, to read and apply its principles, Mike Fischer and Dante Suarez from Trinity

University for believing in me; my kind readers Danielle Warmowski, T. C. Frost, Jean Latting, John Worsham, Helen Worsham, Janine Warmowski, Danielle Supkis-Cheek, Corey Glenn, Dianne Connor, and Mike Connor, for their critiques and good suggestions. In addition, I wish to thank Christi Stanforth for her excellent help with editing and formatting and Eli Miller, whose graphic design skills provided the cover art that brought a smile to my face.

Most of all I want to thank Toby, my husband, with all my heart for putting up with my long days writing and editing, for listening to my doubts and concerns, for reading the drafts, and for continually encouraging me to "get it out there!"

If you have any further questions or want to know more, please email me at moneysmarts4u@gmail.com and look for the launch of the website in a few months, located at www.moneysmarts4u.com.

About the Author

Barbie O'Connor has spent most of her life helping other people manage their money. After seventeen years as a financial advisor at Merrill Lynch, she retired as a vice-president and went on to run an Indy Car team whose car raced in both the 1995 and 1996 Indy 500 races. Most recently she has given seminars on basic money management and served on community boards in San Antonio, Texas.

During her career as a financial advisor she managed over $100 million for her clients and made many presentations on financial management and estate planning for organizations such as Trinity University, St. Mary's University, Merrill Lynch Chairman's Club, Diamond Shamrock, the North San Antonio Chamber of Commerce, the Women's Chamber of Commerce and many others. In addition, the *New York Times*, the *San Antonio Express-News,* WOAI-TV, ESPN, the *Indianapolis Star*, and *Autoweek,* covering topics from auto racing to women's issues to financial management, have interviewed her.

Charitable giving and the management of charitable organizations are topics of particular interest to her. She has served on the boards of the San Antonio Downtown YMCA, the San Antonio Red Cross, Planned Parenthood of San Antonio, Jewish Family Service, the Charity Ball Association, the Ambassadors Circle of the Greehey Children's Cancer Research Center, Alamo Public Telecommunications, and the McNay Art Museum.

At this time her main focus is educating people on how to create and manage their wealth and pass it on to others.